THE
CORNISH
COOK BOOK

A CELEBRATION OF THE AMAZING FOOD & DRINK ON OUR DOORSTEP

The Cornish Cook Book

©2019 Meze Publishing Ltd. All rights reserved.

First edition printed in 2019 in the UK.

ISBN: 978-1-910863-47-3

Compiled by: Jo Mallinder

Written by: Katie Fisher

Photography by: Mike Searle
(www.mikesearlephotography.co.uk)

Edited by: Phil Turner, Chris Brierley

Designed by: Paul Cocker

Contributors: Ruth Alexander, Vanesa Balaj,
Amelia Brownhill, Ceara Gurney, Michael Johnson,
Sarah Koriba, Lauren Nuttall, Paul Stimpson,
Anna Tebble, David Wilson

Cover art: Luke Prest (www.lukeprest.com)

me:ze
PUBLISHING

Published by Meze Publishing Limited
Unit 1b, 2 Kelham Square
Kelham Riverside
Sheffield S3 8SD
Web: www.mezepublishing.co.uk
Telephone: 0114 275 7709
Email: info@mezepublishing.co.uk

CONTENTS

HARBOURING

GREAT THINGS

TUCKED AWAY IN A TINY FORMER NAVAL DOCKYARD, CASTAWAYS'
SECLUDED LOCATION BELIES ITS VIBRANT FOOD, RENOWNED WINE LIST
AND BUZZING ATMOSPHERE.

Tempting and flavoursome food influenced by the Cornish coast is one of many things that make Castaways special. In a restaurant off the beaten track, situated on the Carrick Roads Estuary at Mylor Harbour, there's plenty to choose from when it comes to unique aspects. Despite being something of a hidden gem, Castaways is lively and full of energy thanks to a strong team committed to providing the best service a customer can get.

The team is headed up by general manager Marc and head chef Ben, who love the industry they work in, gleaning ideas and inspiration from both international travel and homegrown products. Scallops, mussels, oysters, lobsters and more can be found in Mylor Harbour where the restaurant is situated, to be washed down with real ale, cider, craft beer and soft drinks produced in Cornwall. When it comes to wine lists, Castaways' has been recognised as amongst the best in the area. Curated with careful attention to detail, the selection is varied and based on visits to vineyards for individual picks. Ben's menu is always tailored to the seasons using the best ingredients he can find, and dishes are freshly prepared, making them easy to alter for vegan and vegetarian customers too.

Whether people come in for a sit-down meal or an evening tipple, they share the open plan vaulted space which lends Castaways its dynamic feel. The restaurant is dog-friendly and attracts a wide range of customers especially at peak times in summer. Castaways' owner Toby spent many of his own childhood summer holidays in this part of Cornwall, and despite a high-flying career in accounting he leapt at the opportunity to take on the restaurant in 2012, and later its sister business, UpperDeck, in Falmouth Marina.

Marc first managed Castaways in 2014 for a couple of years, then went to work for a brewery but missed the place so much that he came back in September 2018. Ben joined in 2018, leading to developments over the following year that pushed the business even further in its evolution. They 'live and breathe' the restaurant, which is evidence of how much effort and enthusiasm is put into the venture every day. All of these things together – personable staff, eclectic menus, Cornish produce, a unique setting, the customers – make Castaways what it is and what it aspires to be.

MOROCCAN-SPICED
CORNISH HAKE

This dish takes local Cornish ingredients and puts a modern North African twist on them, influenced by the fresh simplicity of Ottolenghi.

4 fillets of MSC certified hake

FOR THE HARISSA YOGHURT

500g tub of natural yoghurt

1 generous tsp harissa paste

Pinch of sea salt

FOR THE BUTTERNUT SQUASH

1 butternut squash

Vegetable oil, to coat

FOR THE CORIANDER OIL

1 bunch of coriander

Vegetable oil

Pinch of salt

FOR THE DUKKAH

110g hazelnuts

70g sesame seeds

2 tbsp coriander seeds

2 tbsp cumin seeds

2 tsp black pepper

1 tsp Cornish sea salt

Preheat the oven to 180°c.

FOR THE HARISSA YOGHURT

Transfer the yoghurt into a bowl, add the harissa paste and a pinch of sea salt. Mix until combined then set aside in the fridge.

FOR THE BUTTERNUT SQUASH

Peel the butternut squash, cut in half long ways, deseed, and slice into half-moons. Coat in oil and roast in the oven for 15 minutes at 180°c. Cover the squash in tinfoil so it doesn't burn.

FOR THE CORIANDER OIL

Pick the leaves off a bunch of coriander, place them into the blender and add vegetable oil to just cover the coriander leaves, add a pinch of salt and blend the mix until vibrant green and liquidised.

FOR THE DUKKAH

Roast the hazelnuts on a baking tray in the hot oven for 3 to 4 minutes, then take out. Once cooled, rub the skin off the hazelnuts (easily done in a clean cloth or tea towel). Put them into a food processor, blitz until finely ground then transfer to a bowl.

Place a pan over a medium heat and toast the sesame seeds, coriander seeds and cumin seeds until fragrant and lightly coloured. Do not leave these alone, as if burnt the taste will become bitter and they can catch very quickly! Transfer the seeds into a pestle and mortar and pound until finely crushed. Add all the dukkah ingredients to a bowl, check the seasoning then set aside.

FOR THE HAKE

Pan fry the hake over a high heat, skin side down, and season the flesh of the fish. Once the skin has browned and crisped up, place the pan into the oven at 180°c and cook the fish through for a further 5 minutes.

TO SERVE

Once the fish is in the oven, start to build your dish. Start with the harissa yoghurt, followed by the warmed squash, then place the hake on the top and garnish with dukkah and coriander oil.

Preparation time: approx. 30 minutes | Cooking time: approx. 30 minutes | Serves: 4

HOME

FROM

HOME

FAMILY-FRIENDLY AND FOCUSED ON PERFECTLY PREPARED FOOD, CHARLIE'S IS A CAFÉ AND DELI THAT WILL HIT THE SPOT AT ANY TIME OF DAY.

Rebecca and Daniel opened their first café in 2011 as a husband and wife team, about a year after they had a little boy, so from the very beginning Charlie's was inspired by him in name and in nature as a family-friendly destination for Tintagel locals as well as tourists. They wanted to create somewhere people with young children could go to enjoy great food and drink as well as feeling relaxed and comfortable, which has been reflected in the Cornwall Life awards for Family Dining and then Customer Service that Charlie's won in 2017 and 2018.

Of course the big draw of the café is the top quality food and drink to be found there, from breakfast and lunch to afternoon tea with a tipple if you fancy a beer made in the village, or a sparkling wine from Cornish vineyards. Everything is freshly made and cooked simply but with great care; a prime example is the sourdough bread which Charlie's has become known for, created from a starter nearly as old as the café and proved for 14 hours before being freshly baked every morning.

Rebecca and Daniel have always worked in the hospitality industry, and their experience combined with some fantastic

local and seasonal produce makes each dish – whether it's Eggs Royale, a homemade burger, or a Cornish Cream tea to indulge in – really quite special. Because their food is prepared and cooked in-house there are lots of gluten-free options available too, and whatever you choose the ingredients speak for themselves.

If you just can't get enough of the bread, pickles, jams, chutneys and other treats made at Charlie's, luckily there is a deli section within the café where its own produce sits happily alongside a selection of artisanal delights from nearby producers searched out by Rebecca and Daniel. Parents and children are also happy to discover the play corner, with a miniature kitchen and other toys to explore. The venue itself has an appeal of its own, and there is plenty to remark on in the way of original features from the stone staircase to the slate flooring and wooden beams throughout the 14th century cottages. There is an outdoor courtyard – which is 'a real sun trap' – and a range indoors that everyone makes a beeline for on colder days, making Charlie's a haven for customers looking for homeliness, warmth and great taste for all the family in Tintagel.

HOT CORNISH
CRAB DIP

We think that Cornwall has the tastiest crab in the world and this dip showcases the sweetness and richness fabulously. It's a luxurious dish certain to wow your guests.

50g unsalted butter

1 white onion, finely chopped

1 large clove of garlic, minced

100g brown crab meat

250g cream cheese, softened

100ml sour cream

50ml mayonnaise

¼ tsp Charlie's harissa paste

1 tbsp lemon juice

Salt and plenty of freshly cracked black pepper, to taste

300g white crab meat

TO SERVE

Fresh crusty bread

Fresh breadcrumbs (optional)

Preheat the oven to 180°c.

Melt the butter in a heavy-bottomed pan on a low heat. Slowly sweat the onion and garlic in the butter until soft. Set aside to cool.

When the onion mixture is cool, in a medium-sized mixing bowl, combine it with the brown crab meat, cream cheese, sour cream, mayonnaise, harissa and lemon juice. Season to taste and then gently fold in the white crab meat so as not to break up the nice chunks.

Pour the mixture into a small ovenproof dish and bake for 20 to 25 minutes until heated through and bubbly. Serve the hot dip with fresh bread (the crustier the better). We think our homemade turmeric and onion seed bread is the perfect accompaniment. We also like to sprinkle the baked dip with fresh breadcrumbs for a crunchy topping.

Preparation time: 5 minutes | Cooking time: 25 minutes | Serves: 6+ as a dip or 4 hungry Cornishmen as a snack

A LITTLE

SLICE OF
PARADISE

THE PASSION FOR HORTICULTURE EXTENDS TO MORE THAN THE PLANTS NURTURED AT THE DUCHY OF CORNWALL NURSERY, WHERE INCREASING AMOUNTS OF HOMEGROWN INGREDIENTS ARE TRANSFORMED INTO AWARD-WINNING FOOD.

The café, shop and nursery are intertwined by greenery and good food at the Duchy of Cornwall Nursery. Although the nursery was established during the late 1960s initially to provide saplings for forestry, the café and shop were added far more recently. 2011 saw the new building emerge, which was designed by HRH the Duke of Cornwall and is framed in oak, roofed in cedar and walled with cob. The beautiful and natural exterior reflects the ethos and purpose of the business, drawing people inside to discover a veritable Garden of Eden.

Since the development, business has been flourishing and a trip down the narrow winding lane that seems to lead nowhere is well worthwhile to reach this destination for food and plant lovers alike. There are various spots to enjoy the views and the food at the nursery, including a glasshouse with a locally renowned collection of indoor plants and an outdoor terrace overlooking the Fowey Valley to Restormel Castle. Adjacent to this peaceful setting is the café itself, where breakfast and lunch are served as well as indulgent afternoon and cream teas which feature homemade bread and cakes.

The stunning surroundings of the building give rise to inspiration and a strong sense of place at the Duchy of Cornwall Nursery. "Locally sourced and artisanal produce really means something to us," says general manager Karl. Whether it's dairy from a few miles down the road, fish and seafood landed on the nearest coastline, or herbs from the nursery's own kitchen garden, visitors are spoilt for choice by the abundance of Cornish bounty. The team are excited to be growing more fruit and vegetables on site, in addition to the existing apple orchard, as well as the creation of a bumblebee garden planted only with bee-friendly flora, and open to the public very soon.

With plants and edibles everywhere you look at the Duchy of Cornwall Nursery, running that horticultural thread throughout the business and linking all its aspects together is important, not least so that visitors can take home a bit of what they've seen or tasted from the shop or deli. The nursery has become a destination for the whole family, being dog-friendly and linked to the castle by an English Heritage trail, but above all a place to relax and be inspired by an oasis of homegrown Cornish goodness.

DUCHY *of* CORNWALL

Nursery
Café & Shop
Tel 01208 872668

Monday–Saturday 9.00am–5.00pm
Sunday 10.00am–5.00pm
Café closes at 4.30pm

This building
was opened by
Their Royal Highnesses
The Duke and Duchess of Cornwall
12th July 2011

DUCHY of CORNWALL
NURSERY

DUCHY of CORNWALL NURSERY

Hedging

Perennials & Grasses

SLOW-COOKED
CORNISH OXTAIL PIE

*This recipe came about after one of our other oxtail dishes went down so well in
the café. Using many of the same ingredients, this reinvention gives our customers
a new spin on something we know they love.*

FOR THE OXTAIL

400g onion

40g garlic

200g celery

4 bay leaves

10g thyme

10g rosemary

Salt and pepper

1.2kg oxtail (including bones)

1 litre beef stock

FOR THE PASTRY

120g suet

240g self-raising flour

2 tsp horseradish

Pinch of salt

FOR THE ROASTED
VEGETABLES

550g carrots

400g shallots

2 tbsp sunflower oil

Salt and pepper

FOR THE PIES

150ml red wine

1 egg

FOR THE
CAULIFLOWER PURÉE

1 small cauliflower

500ml milk

FOR THE GARNISH

80g leek

12 leaves of sage

TO SERVE

80g watercress

FOR THE OXTAIL

Preheat the oven to 160°c. Roughly chop half the onion, garlic, celery and herbs, then season and place in a deep roasting tray. Add the oxtail and enough beef stock to cover the meat. Cover the tray and cook for 2 hours until the meat falls away from the bone. Remove the oxtail from the liquid and when cool enough separate the meat from bones. Sieve and cool the liquor, removing the fat when solidified.

FOR THE PASTRY

Mix the suet, flour, horseradish and a pinch of salt in a bowl then add water to bind the pastry together. Set aside in the fridge to firm up.

FOR THE ROASTED VEGETABLES

Peel then top and tail the carrots and cut each one lengthways or into quarters if large. Peel and halve the shallots lengthways. Toss the carrots with seasoned oil in a roasting tray. They will take the same time as the pies so place them into the oven at that point, and after 20 minutes add the shallots, give everything a good mix, then return to the oven.

FOR THE PIES

Roll out the chilled pastry into four rounds big enough to line four individual pie moulds with four lids (I like to use a muffin tray) then place in the fridge. Finely dice the remaining onion, garlic, celery, thyme and rosemary. Sweat them down in a pan, when soft add the red wine, then increase the heat and reduce to a syrupy consistency. Add the oxtail, bay leaves and enough of the skimmed stock to cover everything. Bring to the boil and allow the filling to thicken. Fill each pie case, add the lid, crimp and egg wash the tops. The pies are now ready to go into the oven for approximately 45 minutes (along with the roast vegetables as above).

FOR THE CAULIFLOWER PURÉE

Remove the outer leaves and cut the cauliflower into quarters. Simmer these in milk until cooked through, then drain without discarding the liquid. Place the cauliflower in a food processor, blend until smooth, adding a little milk as needed to achieve the correct consistency. Taste and season.

FOR THE GARNISH

Top, tail and finely slice the leek. They must be dry so they can be deep fried in hot oil until crispy. Remove from the oil when just golden and place on a paper towel to drain. Do the same with sage leaves.

TO SERVE

Place the pies and caramelised vegetables neatly on the plate, add a generous spoonful of the warm cauliflower purée with a nest of washed watercress on top. Scatter some crispy leeks and sage over the pie. The remaining stock could also be thickened and used for extra gravy if you like. Enjoy!

Preparation time: approx. 1 hour | Cooking time: 2 hours 30 minutes | Serves: 4

A CORNISH OASIS

SINCE HUSBAND AND WIFE TEAM DAVE AND NATALIE TOOK ON DUKE ST. CAFÉ IN NEWLYN, BUSINESS HAS BEEN BOOMING AT THE HEART OF THE TOWN AND ITS COMMUNITY.

Dave and Nat grew up in Cornwall, both in villages close to the busy fishing port of Newlyn, and worked in the catering industry leading up to their first venture into café ownership, on Duke Street in the town closest to their childhood homes. In the few years since then, their small business has flourished and developed with surprising speed – even the couple themselves hadn't expected to become so busy so quickly – thanks to great quality food and a homely environment. They have won Bronze in the 2019 Cornish Tourism Awards for Best Café, and established Duke St. Café as a hub for the community where regulars come in every day and customers know staff by names and faces.

Creating a welcoming atmosphere and producing delicious food and drink are equally important to the team at Duke St. Café. The breakfast, brunch and lunch options are built around traditional British flavours and great Cornish produce; everything is sourced from within the county where possible and most travels less than five miles to the kitchen, including fish and seafood landed at Newlyn. Good relationships with these suppliers and producers have enabled the café to keep its offering affordable while ensuring the quality of each ingredient.

Pulling the strings in the kitchen, Lauren and Chantelle deliver everything from homemade cakes to the inspired specials that add a special something to the menu. They balance flavour with accessibility as well as heading up the team. More than just staff members, they also get involved with fundraising and events in the town, and 2019 marked the third summer the whole crew have worked together, a pretty unique achievement and one that's testament to Duke St. Café's atmosphere for both customers and staff. "We're trying to create a little oasis here away from the day to day stresses of busy lives," says Dave, "so that anyone can come in, relax and have a chat over our lovely coffee and cake."

With two little boys and a second business over at Trewidden Gardens, where they run the tearoom, Dave and Nat have a lot on their plates, but luckily – with the hard work of a loyal team and the bounty of Cornwall surrounding them – at Duke St. Café those platefuls are never less than delicious!

NEWLYN SMOKED HADDOCK, BACON AND LEEK CHOWDER

This is one of our most popular dishes here, a real favourite with locals and visitors alike. If you can't get haddock you can use any smoked white fish to give the same lovely taste!

1 white onion

1 stick of celery

2 medium leeks

3 rashers of bacon

2 tbsp vegetable or olive oil

2 large or 3 smaller white potatoes

1 litre fish or chicken stock

140g sweetcorn (equal to a small tin)

500g smoked haddock

200ml double cream

Small handful of chopped parsley

Black pepper

1 lemon, sliced into wedges

Finely chop the onion, celery and leeks. Dice the bacon and add to a big saucepan with the oil on a medium to high heat until bacon is lightly browned. Turn down the heat slightly and add the onion, leeks and celery. Cook for around 5 minutes until softened; keep stirring to avoid it catching on the bottom of the pan. While the mixture is cooking, peel and chop the potatoes roughly into 1cm cubes and add to the pan.

Next add the stock and sweetcorn, bring to the boil then simmer for around 15 minutes or until the potatoes are just cooked. Meanwhile, take the skin off the haddock and roughly chop the fish into 1cm pieces. If you want, leave some pieces a little bigger to pan fry and place on top when serving it looks lovely; leave those to one side and add the rest of the fish to the pan. After a few minutes the fish will break apart easily, meaning it's cooked. At that point take either a stick blender or a potato masher and blend half of the mixture, leaving the other half chunky, to thicken the chowder while giving it some texture.

Add the double cream and chopped parsley, keeping some back for garnish, and gently cook for 3 to 4 minutes. Season with pepper to taste. You shouldn't need much salt, if any, as the fish and bacon add the saltiness. If the chowder is too thick loosen with a bit of water. If you have left some fish to put on top, put two tablespoons of oil in a frying pan on medium-high and cook the pieces for 2 minutes on each side until the fish turns opaque. If you overcook it, the pieces will fall apart.

Put a few ladles of chowder in a bowl, top with the pan fried fish, a sprinkle of parsley and a wedge of lemon then enjoy!

Preparation time: 10 minutes | Cooking time: 20-25 minutes | Serves: 6-8

TWO I'S ARE

BETTER THAN ONE

BY DAY, EDIE'S KITCHEN IS A COSY CAFÉ SERVING BRUNCH AND LUNCH, BUT COME EVENING IT TRANSFORMS INTO AN ELEGANT BISTRO: WHICHEVER YOU CHOOSE, WHAT TIES IT ALL TOGETHER IS THE QUALITY OF THE FOOD AND THE COMMITMENT OF THE FAMILY WHO RUN AND OWN THE CARLYON BAY RESTAURANT.

The clue to this restaurant's family friendly, welcoming vibe is in its name. Edie's kitchen was so called after the the co-owners Kelly and Nigel Brown's daughter. A daughter who now works with them part time. Two green 'I's in the name acknowledge the addition of their second daughter, Iris, into the family business which was established in late 2017. Having worked in restaurants across the UK and in Australia, for the likes of Raymond Blanc and Bill Granger, chef Nigel and front of house manager Kelly brought their expertise to Nigel's home county, where he had always wanted to set up a restaurant of his own.

Their location in Carlyon Bay has "year-round appeal" says Kelly, and is open throughout Cornwall's usual off-season because of this, something its owners love because it means they get to know local people as well as welcoming new faces. A typical day at Edie's kicks things off with the brunch menu, which is joined by a prix fixe menu from midday that allows customers plenty of choice between indulgent breakfast dishes and luxurious lunches. As the evening draws in, candles are lit, lights are dimmed and music softens to create a wonderful bistro setting reflective of its quality food offering.

"Even though I've worked in fine dining restaurants in the past, I'm only interested in creating, simple, elegant, unfussy dishes that will appeal to everyone!" says Nigel. His influences stem from the chefs he's worked with to produce a fusion between classic French and modern British cooking, with a little Aussie café culture thrown in. Nigel and Wes, his sous chef, bounce ideas around for the ever-evolving menu which they update every five weeks, keeping even regular guests intrigued.

From the restaurant – with its clean, bright décor and wooden shelves laden with cook books to flick through – diners can see into the open kitchen where dishes are being freshly prepared and cooked with the best ingredients to be found. Kelly and restaurant manager Katherine ensure a warm and friendly atmosphere pervades the space, encouraged by laid-back service and chat between staff and guests so everyone feels relaxed. "We love what we do here," says Kelly, "and just want to keep moving forward. Perhaps one day we'll open a second venue for Iris!'

We really hope so.

DOUBLE BAKED
CHEESE SOUFFLÉ

This dish was on our menu from the first day we opened. It is the only starter that has stayed consistently on our menu even though we change them every five to six weeks. We simply change the flavour of the cheese! It's super popular as a starter but people with lighter appetites like to eat one with a side of our homemade chunky hand cut chips.

FOR THE SOUFFLÉ

Soft butter, for greasing the moulds

100g panko breadcrumbs

32g unsalted butter

40g plain flour

180ml milk

160g good quality cheddar cheese

1 tsp Dijon mustard

2 egg yolks

2 egg whites

Salt and pepper

FOR THE WHITE WINE CREAM

200ml white wine

1 banana shallot, peeled and halved

3 cloves of garlic, peeled

2 sprigs of thyme

2 bay leaves

200ml double cream

TO SERVE

Few handfuls of spinach, wilted

1 Braeburn apple

Bunch of watercress

Drizzle of olive, rapeseed or lemon oil (your choice)

FOR THE SOUFFLÉ

Firstly, preheat the oven to 160°c.

Brush the moulds with the soft butter, giving them a good coating, then add a tablespoon of the panko breadcrumbs to each and move the moulds around to ensure they are completely coated in the breadcrumbs. Pop the moulds in the freezer.

Gently heat the butter in a medium pan, then once it's melted and slightly bubbling add the flour and stir in. Cook until the mixture turns a sandy colour, then add a third of the milk and stir to combine. Keep adding the milk a third at a time, ensuring the mix is well beaten to create a smooth mixture. Add the cheese of your choice, remove from the heat and mix until all the cheese has melted. Add the Dijon mustard and stir through, followed by the egg yolks. Set aside and leave to cool to room temperature. Meanwhile, whisk the egg whites to stiff peaks in a free-standing mixer, adding a small pinch of salt as you whisk. Using a metal spoon, fold the whipped whites into the cooled soufflé mixture a third at a time.

Take the moulds out of the freezer and fill each one two thirds full, place in a roasting tray and fill the tray with water until it reaches halfway up the moulds. Place in the preheated oven and cook for 25 minutes. Once cooked, remove from the oven and set aside until cool enough to handle, then gently ease the soufflés out of the moulds. Set aside until needed.

FOR THE WHITE WINE CREAM

Place the wine, shallot, garlic, thyme and bay leaves in a pan. Bring to the boil and reduce the liquid by half. Add the double cream, bring back to the boil then reduce to a simmer for 5 minutes. Pass through a sieve to end up with a smooth sauce.

TO SERVE

Preheat the oven to 180°c. Place the soufflés on a tray and warm through in the oven for 6 to 8 minutes. Warm the sauce and pour some into the serving bowls. Add a small amount of wilted spinach in the centre and sit the soufflé on top. Finely slice the apple into matchsticks, mix with a little of the watercress and dress with oil of your choice. Sit the salad on top of the soufflé and serve.

Preparation time: 30 minutes | Cooking time: 25 minutes | Serves: 6

THE BISCUITS THAT

FAIR WELL

FURNISS IS THE OLDEST AND MOST CHERISHED CORNISH BISCUIT BRAND, STEEPED IN LOCAL TRADITION AND SYNONYMOUS WITH NOSTALGIC CORNISH SUMMER HOLIDAYS.

The story begins in Cornwall, back in 1886, when master baker John Cooper Furniss opened his first teashop in the centre of Truro. Every night he would work into the small hours, preparing delicious gingerbread and celebrated fairings ready to serve fresh the next day. His passion for using the best local ingredients and exacting attention to detail quickly secured the Furniss teashop a reputation for serving up the tastiest biscuits in town, and orders began to pour in from surrounding areas.

The small business has continued to flourish ever since, and in 2006 Furniss became part of the locally owned Proper Cornish Food Company. Chairman Phil along with fellow shareholders Chris and Gerald make up the close-knit core team, who work hard to preserve the heritage of the favourite Cornish brand. The bakers create Furniss products with the same passion that John Cooper Furniss had, including the Original Cornish Fairing, a unique biscuit which was originally given as a gift to loved ones at Cornish fairs in the 19th century. Rather aptly, it remains Furniss' most loved product, and has even earned its own trademark. The fairing won Silver in the 2018 Taste of the West Awards, while its indulgent companion, Furniss' Cornish Clotted Cream Shortbread with Strawberries, scooped Gold.

While traditional and heritage sit at the heart of the company's success, the team at Furniss aren't afraid of adding a few modern twists and love experimenting with new flavours and combinations. Their ginger biscuits come in a range of flavours, from dark chocolate to blossom honey and spiced lemon. Being proud Cornishmen, Phil and his team use local ingredients for their bakes whenever possible. The award-winning shortbread is made with clotted cream and butter from Trewithen Dairy, a family-run farm only a few miles from the bakery.

With a historic connection to the spice trade and plans to introduce a Sicilian Lemon Shortbread to the range very soon, it's easy to see that – while proudly holding the badge for Cornwall's favourite biscuit – Furniss is also inspired by authentic flavours and ingredients that cross borders. Its luxury biscuits adorn the shelves of Cornish shops and cafés, but can also be found nationwide, so wherever in the country you call home, your biscuit tin will never have to go empty again!

ORIGINAL CORNISH FAIRINGS
AND PASSION FRUIT CHEESECAKE

At Furniss we love this particular recipe because of the contrast between the beautiful passion fruit zing in the filling and our famous artisanal Original Cornish Fairing crumb for the base: just mouth-watering! Other biscuits in our range make great substitutes if you fancy a different base flavour; why not give it a go with our Original Cornish Gingerbread?

450g Furniss Original Cornish Fairings

100g butter, melted

7g gelatine

30ml hot water

9 small passion fruit (to yield 140g)

500g full-fat cream cheese

250g double cream

155g caster sugar

Crumble the Furniss Original Cornish Fairings either by hand or in a blender, then add the melted butter. Fold it into the crumb then transfer the mixture into a 20-25cm loose-bottomed or spring-form cake tin, using the back of a spoon to press it down firmly and evenly. Place this in the fridge while you create the filling.

Dissolve the gelatine (powdered or otherwise) in the hot water, stirring gently, then set aside to cool. Halve each passion fruit, spoon out the centres into a sieve and use the back of a spoon to press the liquid through into a clean bowl. Add the cream cheese, double cream, caster sugar and set gelatine to another mixing bowl and whip everything together. Once the passion fruit has been weighed out, pour it into the bowl while blending, and stop when the mixture is stiff. Remove the base from the fridge, spoon the firm cheesecake mixture into the tin and smooth over with a clean spoon.

The cheesecake can be finished with a light scattering of any remaining passion fruit pulp and seeds. This beautiful dessert with a wonderful Cornish twist can be served with or without a jus or cream!

Preparation time: 55 minutes | Chilling time: 2-3 hours minimum (ideally overnight) | Serves: 4-6

LIFE'S A

GYLLY BEACH

BY DAY, BY NIGHT, FOR ICE CREAM, FRESHLY BAKED BREAD, CLASSIC SEASIDE LUNCHES OR CONTEMPORARY DINING: GYLLY BEACH CAFÉ HAS IT ALL!

Gylly Beach Café opened in 2000 and has made the most of its wonderful location on Falmouth's famous Gyllyngvase Beach ever since. Owners Simon and Viv first transformed the venue into a popular eatery, which has gone from strength to strength as the business has evolved over the years. In 2008 the café got a makeover thanks to a huge refurbishment, and eight years later the Bakery on the Beach was created to provide all the breads, cakes, pastries and other fresh bakes for the café menu and for general sale.

Day-to-day running of the café is managed by Amy, Mark and Dale who thrive on a full house: an important trait at Gylly Beach because it's open from morning till evening every day of the year except December 25th! This commitment to catering for anyone and everyone extends to every aspect of the business. They step away from the expected and don't provide WiFi. "We want people to appreciate the view over the beach," says Amy, "and to embrace interacting with each other when they visit Gylly Café."

The overall style is modern British, with a big emphasis on fish and seafood given the location, moving through seaside classics to contemporary dining over the day. The kitchen team make absolutely everything in-house using some of Cornwall's finest ingredients; they work with a local forager and back door fishermen with lobster pots that can be seen from the restaurant! The whole café team pride themselves on using local and seasonal produce.

This ethos is reflected in the expansive windows, the spacious awning for outside seating in all weathers, and the events that run throughout the year. Gylly Beach Café hosts live music every Sunday evening, serving its renowned 'Roast on the Coast' over the winter months. From Easter until the end of summer alongside their restaurant menu, there is an open air fire pit on the veranda every evening, serving prime cuts of local meat, with a seafood bar where customers can choose their own fish and shellfish.

The team's laid-back style and friendly welcome combine perfectly with their experience and genuine love for the café and its stunning setting, creating a multi-faceted business that's a real favourite with its visitors. There are plans to expand their success through the bakery, which has started providing other nearby businesses with its goods, and a takeaway element to their food so customers can get even closer to the beautiful Gyllyngvase Beach every time they visit.

KOREV BEER BATTERED HADDOCK, TRIPLE COOKED CHIPS, TARTARE SAUCE

A British classic should be kept simple to not spoil the simplicity of a real favourite. We make our batter from Korev lager to keep it light and fresh with a crisp bubbly texture that wraps around a fillet of Cornish haddock. The variety of potato used is just as important; in this recipe I've chosen Maris Piper which is dry and low in sugars so doesn't colour too quickly while cooking.

FOR THE TARTARE SAUCE

3 egg yolks
1 tsp English mustard
1 tsp white wine vinegar
250ml rapeseed oil
2 gherkins
1 tbsp Lilliput capers
1 lemon

FOR THE TRIPLE COOKED CHIPS

6 large Maris Piper potatoes
Rapeseed oil, for frying

FOR THE BATTERED FISH

568ml (1 pint) Korev Cornish Lager
350g self-raising flour
Handful of chopped curly parsley
Pinch of salt
4 fillets of haddock

Start by making a mayonnaise. Whisk together the egg yolks, English mustard and vinegar then slowly add the 250ml of rapeseed oil until the mixture has emulsified. Dice the gherkins and add these to the mayonnaise with the capers. Halve the lemon, set one half aside and squeeze the juice from the other half. Add the lemon juice to the tartare sauce and stir to combine everything.

Peel the potatoes and cut into chip-sized pieces. Cook these in boiling water until tender, then drain and put in the freezer briefly to dry them out. Meanwhile, heat the rapeseed oil for frying to 120°c and cook the chilled chips until soft. At this stage they won't colour, just soften. Remove the chips from the oil and set aside to drain until required.

FOR THE BATTER

Whisk the beer and flour together until there are no lumps. Add the chopped parsley and a pinch of salt. Dip the haddock into the batter to coat each fillet, then heat the oil to 180°c and gently drop the fish in to cook for 4 to 6 minutes. Remove and set aside to drain. Reduce the oil temperature down to 120°c then drop the chips into the oil and cook until golden brown.

TO SERVE

Place the chips on the plates and top with a haddock fillet, a dollop of tartare sauce, garden peas if you like and a wedge of lemon each.

Preparation time: 20 minutes | Cooking time: 20 minutes | Serves: 4

WOOD-SMOKED PORK BELLY

Primrose Herd pork is a traditional and non-intensive approach to animal husbandry producing excellent marbling in the meat, a good meat and fat ratio, and a more developed flavour. The belly is cold smoked over beech wood and adds a real nutty finish to this dish, which is served with a bacon hash, fried duck egg and apple cider chutney.

FOR THE PORK BELLY

Equal quantities of carrot, onion, celery and garlic (to fill the roasting tray)

Few sprigs of thyme

Few bay leaves

1.5kg smoked pork belly (from Primrose Herd)

568ml (1 pint) good Cornish cider (we use Cornish Orchards)

284ml (½ pint) chicken stock

FOR THE BACON HASH

400g baking potatoes

250g smoked streaky bacon

75g shallots

2 tsp sage, finely chopped

FOR THE FRIED DUCK EGGS

4 duck eggs

Dash of rapeseed oil

TO SERVE

Halzephron Apple and Garlic Chutney

Bunch of watercress

FOR THE PORK BELLY

Preheat the oven to 160°c. Roughly chop all the trivet vegetables (leaving all the skins on as this adds flavour) then scatter them with the thyme and bay into a high-sided oven tray. Place the pork belly on top of the vegetables then cover everything with the cider and chicken stock. Cover the whole tin with greaseproof paper and then again with tin foil. Place in the preheated oven for 4 hours or until tender.

Once the pork belly is cooked, leave it to rest while you assemble the dish. To get a cleaner cut, you can press the belly between two baking trays with a weight on top while it cools.

FOR THE BACON HASH

Place the baking potatoes in the oven and cook until just underdone. Scoop the flesh out of the skins and grate the potatoes while still warm. Grill the bacon until crisp, chop into small pieces and add to the grated potato. Finally dice the shallot then gently fry in oil. Add the chopped sage, then combine the shallot mixture with the potato mixture. Mould the hash to your desired shape, and warm through if needed when ready to plate.

TO FINISH

Pan fry the duck eggs and then portion the pork. Sit the belly alongside the hash on the plate, top with a fried duck egg, then add a spoonful of chutney and a bunch of fresh watercress to finish.

Preparation time: 1 hour 10 minutes | Cooking time: 4 hours | Serves: 4

BLUEBERRY
AND LIME CAKE

*This cake tastes like cheesecake thanks to the soured cream and luxurious
topping. It's also great with raspberries and lemon; just replace the blueberries and
lime with the same quantities. A really popular summer time cake at Gylly Café.*

FOR THE CAKE

175g butter, softened

175g caster sugar

225g plain flour

15g baking powder

3 medium-sized eggs

*½ tsp vanilla paste or 1 vanilla pod, split
and seeds scraped out*

100ml soured cream

120g blueberries

FOR THE ICING

150g cream cheese

110g double cream

30g icing sugar

15ml lime juice

1 lime, zested

Fresh blueberries, for decoration

FOR THE CAKE

Grease and line a round 20cm cake tin. Preheat oven 175°c.

Cream the butter and sugar until light and fluffy using a wooden spoon, hand-held whisk or electric mixer. In a separate bowl, sift the flour and baking powder together. Slowly add the eggs and vanilla paste or seeds to the creamed butter and sugar, alternating this with a spoonful of sifted flour and baking powder, until incorporated. Fold in the remaining flour and baking powder. Add the soured cream and stir until combined. Gently mix in half of the fruit, then transfer the mixture to the prepared cake tin. Scatter the remaining berries over the cake. Bake for approximately 1 hour or until firm to touch.

Baker's tip: this cake can be made with frozen fruit. Defrost slightly before mixing in, so the berries hold their shape but don't freeze the cake batter.

FOR THE ICING

Beat the cream cheese until soft then beat in the cream. Beat in the icing sugar (sift this beforehand if needed) until the mixture is stiff but spreadable. Beat in the lime juice and half of the zest, then spread the icing over the top of the cooled cake. Scatter the remaining zest onto the cake and top with fresh blueberries to finish.

Preparation time: approx. 15 minutes | Cooking time: approx. 1 hour | Serves: 6-8

ESCAPE TO

THE EDGE

LEWINNICK LODGE IS NESTLED ON THE VERY EDGE OF THE SPECTACULAR PENTIRE HEADLAND, PUTTING PANORAMIC SEA VIEWS AT THE HEART OF ITS PEOPLE-FOCUSED EXPERIENCES.

Historically a smuggler's den and a lobster hold, Lewinnick Lodge is still very much connected with its beautiful location through food and design. The ambience throughout the restaurant is enhanced by the venue's fantastic location on the clifftop, offering spectacular ocean views and lending the terrace a Mediterranean feel when the Cornish sun is shining. Whether a storm brings clouds scudding across the horizon, or the sun is setting over a calm sea, wherever you choose to enjoy a drink or bite to eat at Lewinnick, the panoramas are inescapable!

From the dog-friendly bar to the fireside seating and open air terrace, the dining options at Lewinnick are both inspiring and cosy. This approach is reflected in the menu, which emphasises fresh fish and seafood in the specials, offered alongside dishes including polenta-crusted squid with a Vietnamese salad, and succulent steak from local Cornish farms. Head chef Anthony Theobald describes his food as "vibrant and honest" and cooks in a way that revolves around treating quality ingredients with respect.

The business as a whole uses lots of Cornish ingredients and suppliers to furnish every aspect of the Lodge with quality products, including organic toiletries and soft furnishings in the 17 individually designed bedrooms. Sustainability is really important at Lewinnick – evidenced by a recent Silver Green Tourism Award – so the Lodge features a bore hole pump, solar panels, a biomass boiler and policies to cut down on single-use plastics across the board.

Pete and Jacqui Fair bought the venue in the 1990s and made it their mission to create somewhere special to stay and eat, and today their son Daniel follows in those footsteps to keep the business moving forwards and improving. The business continues to grow organically through word of mouth, based on the experiences customers enjoy there. Daniel cites their talented and hard-working team as key to this success; everyone is focused on the little details that make every visit that little bit more special.

"This is my parent's life's work," he says, "so the popularity of Lewinnick Lodge and the beautiful dining and guest experiences we have here are really a testament to them."

CORNISH YARG,
LEEK AND MUSTARD SAUSAGES

*"After working in South Wales for nine years, I thought that wild garlic Cornish yarg would
be a great change from using Caerphilly cheese in the classic Glamorgan sausage. We
serve these with mustard mash, tenderstem broccoli and a tomato and tarragon dressing.
A British classic with a Cornish twist!" – Anthony Theobald, head chef.*

FOR THE SAUSAGES

2 leeks

25g butter

250g wild garlic yarg, grated

175g fresh white breadcrumbs

2 tbsp fresh tarragon, chopped

2 tbsp fresh parsley, chopped

3 egg yolks

1 tbsp wholegrain mustard

Cornish sea salt and ground black pepper

100g plain flour

2 eggs

100g panko breadcrumbs

FOR THE DRESSING

200ml cold-pressed rapeseed oil

50ml white wine vinegar

150g tomato ketchup

5 drops of Tabasco sauce

100g shallots, finely diced

20g tarragon, finely snipped

5g chervil, finely snipped

5g chives, finely snipped

FOR THE MASH

1kg Maris Piper potatoes

250ml double cream

100g butter

1 tbsp wholegrain mustard

FOR THE SAUSAGES

Remove the tops and outer skins of the leeks, split them long ways and wash
carefully, then finely slice. Sweat the sliced leeks in the butter until soft, but not
coloured, which takes about 8 to 10 minutes. Transfer the leeks into a colander to
cool and let the excess moisture drip out. In a separate bowl, combine the grated
yarg, fresh breadcrumbs and herbs. In another bowl, beat the egg yolks with the
mustard, salt and pepper. Once the leeks are cold, mix them with the cheese and
egg mixtures. Divide into twelve equal portions, shape into sausages and put into
the freezer for 20 to 30 minutes to set.

To finish the sausages, set up a breadcrumbing station with three tubs or bowls –
one containing the flour, one containing the eggs whisked with a pinch of salt, and
one containing the panko breadcrumbs – then coat the chilled sausages one by
one in that order. When they have all been dipped in flour, egg, and breadcrumbs,
refrigerate the sausages until needed.

FOR THE DRESSING

Combine the rapeseed oil and white wine vinegar in a bowl with a pinch of salt
and a couple of twists of pepper. Use a small whisk to emulsify the mixture before
adding the ketchup, Tabasco, shallots and herbs. Stir gently then taste and adjust the
seasoning if necessary. The sauce is ready to use right away, but can be kept in an
airtight container in the fridge for up to three days. Return to room temperature to
serve.

FOR THE MASH

Peel and dice the potatoes into 5cm cubes then wash until the starch is all gone (this
will stop the potatoes going gluey once cooked). Place in a saucepan, cover with
cold water, season, bring to the boil and then gently simmer until the potatoes are
just cooked. Pour the potatoes into a colander and leave to steam so they dry as
much as possible. In the meantime, put the cream and butter into a pan and bring
to the boil. Pass the potatoes through a ricer and gradually add the cream mixture
bit by bit until incorporated. To finish, add the wholegrain mustard and season with
Cornish sea salt.

TO FINISH

Deep fry the sausages in hot oil until golden and serve with the mustard mash, some
steamed tenderstem broccoli, the tomato dressing and a garnish of pea shoots.

Preparation time: approx. 1 hour | Cooking time: approx. 30 minutes | Serves: 6

CHOCOLATE DELICE
AND HAZELNUT MACAROONS

"This dish was created purely from my love of macaroons and the combination of hazelnuts, dark chocolate and coffee."

FOR THE DELICE

150ml full-fat milk

330ml double cream

2 free-range eggs

340g 70% cocoa chocolate, chopped

1 tin of condensed milk, boiled for 3 hours then cooled

FOR THE MACAROONS

275g icing sugar

200g ground almonds

75g hazelnuts, roasted and ground

200g egg whites

250g sugar

60ml water

FOR THE
CHOCOLATE GANACHE

300ml double cream

300g dark chocolate

FOR THE WHITE
CHOCOLATE SOIL

200g sugar

75ml water

80g white chocolate

2g salt

TO SERVE

Handful of hazelnuts, roasted and chopped

Callestick Farm espresso ice cream

FOR THE DELICE

Put the milk and cream in a pan and gently bring to the boil. Meanwhile, whisk the eggs in a bowl then pour the hot cream mixture over the eggs, whisking continuously to cook the eggs. Add the chopped chocolate and keep mixing until smooth. Pour into round metal moulds, filling halfway to the top. Keep the remaining third of the chocolate mixture in a warm place so it stays liquid, and put the moulds into the fridge to set. Once set, use a melon baller to remove a scoop from the middle of each delice and fill with the condensed milk caramel (the result of the boiled and cooled condensed milk) so it's level. Pour a little of the warm delice mixture over the top to cover the caramel and chill in fridge until needed.

FOR THE MACAROONS

In a food processor, blend the icing sugar, ground almonds, ground hazelnuts and half of the egg whites to a paste. Put the sugar and water into a pan and gradually bring up to 118°c; when the sugar syrup reaches 108°c start to whisk the remaining 100g of egg whites in a separate bowl. By the time the sugar reaches 118°c the egg whites will be ready for the sugar syrup; slowly pour it over the whipped egg whites while whisking. This will cook the egg whites and become a smooth and glossy Italian meringue mixture. Fold the almond paste and meringue together until combined, then transfer the mixture into a piping bag and pipe 2½ cm rounds onto silicone non-stick mats, making sure there is enough space between each one so they don't merge together. Leave to rest for 15 to 20 minutes then bake in the oven at 130°c for 15 to 17 minutes. Leave to cool completely.

FOR THE CHOCOLATE GANACHE

In the meantime, make the ganache by heating the cream and pouring it over the chocolate, stirring continuously until the chocolate is all melted and smooth. Put half of the ganache in a piping bag to fill the macaroons, and the other half into a container. Keep this room temperature for garnishing.

FOR THE WHITE CHOCOLATE SOIL

Put the sugar and water into a pan and cook on a high heat to 135°c. Remove from the heat and immediately add the white chocolate, whisking continuously until all the liquid has crystalised. Put the mixture into a container and leave to cool.

TO SERVE

Add a swipe of ganache to the plate, remove the delice from the metal ring using heat to loosen it (a blow torch is good for this) and place over the ganache. Crumble white chocolate soil over the top, add one macaroon, some roasted chopped hazelnuts and a ball of espresso ice cream to finish.

Preparation time: 1-2 hours | Cooking time: 3 hours 30 minutes | Serves: 6

ESCAPE
TO THE
COUNTRY

BEAUTIFUL SURROUNDINGS AND RELAXED DINING WITH A NOSE-TO-TAIL
ETHOS BRINGS THE OUTSIDE IN AND VICE VERSA AT PENROSE KITCHEN.

The award-winning restaurant Penrose Kitchen is something of a hidden gem, on the outskirts of Truro amidst lily ponds and acres of grazing deer. Reflecting their idyllic rural location, owners Ben and Samantha have developed a style of food and drink that celebrates Cornwall's finest ingredients from individual farms and suppliers. Being off the beaten track can be hard work, but since it was established in August 2016 Penrose Kitchen has steadily gained a reputation across the whole county thanks to word of mouth recommendation and social media. "We're still evolving," says Ben, "and are always just aiming for people to appreciate what we do."

Husband and wife Ben and Samantha have "lived and breathed the industry since day dot" with Ben working in the kitchens of the Savoy and Le Gavroche straight out of college, and Samantha working her way up to restaurant manager at top restaurants in Cheltenham and Cornwall. After Ben moved to Cornwall to work for Rick Stein, the couple left the county briefly but missed it so much they promptly moved back! They realised that both of them wanted the same thing when it came to opening their own business, and the opportunity

arose with a former tearoom going up for lease. They initially turned it down, but then a change of heart meant getting the place ready in just two weeks, enlisting family to help transform the venue into a light and airy space, complete with outdoor terrace to enjoy in warmer weather.

The lunch and dinner menus at Penrose Kitchen are 'elemental' in the sense that dishes are developing according to the weather that day…like surfers, Ben and Samantha are always listening to the forecast and preparing accordingly! Rain or shine dictates the fruit and vegetables they choose to work with, and also the morning's catch from the fish supplier. Ben likes to use as much of the animal as possible in exciting ways; his braised ox tongue is a best-seller.

Turning people's expectations on their heads is something Penrose Kitchen does with unique style and relaxed elegance. The establishment is also the first restaurant in Cornwall so far to join the Carbon Free Dining Initiative. The drive to embody excellence is evident in all aspects of the venture, from its out of the way but stunning setting to the quality of the food and its proudly unpretentious Cornish roots.

CORNISH SURF
AND TURF

This dish is based upon my fondness for blending fish and meat and to create a surf and turf dish with a twist. Our restaurant is built upon the foundation of using local produce, being bold and innovative with our creations and blending with passion.

300g Cornish earlies (potatoes)

Fine table salt

2 small lemon sole, skinned and filleted

110g Cornish unsalted butter

10 seedless red grapes

200g lamb's liver

½ lemon, juiced

1 large pinch of good quality saffron (Cheshire or Cornish organic)

5ml vegetable oil

300g baby spinach, washed

Wash the potatoes in warm water to remove excess dirt and loose skin. Fill a saucepan with fresh cold water, add a pinch of salt and put the potatoes in. Bring to the boil then simmer gently until cooked through. If the potatoes are done they will slide easily off a knife. Drain and add 20g of the butter and a pinch of salt to the pan, then cover with foil and or a lid to keep hot until needed.

Preheat the oven to 180°c. Lay the lemon sole fillets flat on a chopping board skin side down and season lightly with salt. Roll each one up, but not too tightly to ensure even cooking. Lightly grease a flat baking tray with 10g of soft butter and place the fillets and grapes on it. Bake in the oven for 5 minutes.

Place a griddle pan on the stove and let it heat for about 2 minutes. Season the liver with a little vegetable oil and salt then cook for approximately 1 minute on each side. Remove from the heat and allow the meat to rest.

Put the lemon juice and the saffron into a small saucepan, gently heat and then stir in the remaining 80g of butter. Add a good pinch of salt and set aside.

Heat a small frying pan and add the vegetable oil. Place the spinach in the pan with a pinch of salt and lightly toss until wilted. Remove and drain off any excess water.

Remove the fish from the oven. Arrange the spinach in the centre of a warm plate. Place the fish fillets on top of the spinach and arrange the potatoes around the fish. Thinly slice the pink liver and lay in between the fish. Place a grape on each fish fillet, pour over the butter sauce and serve.

Preparation time: 5 minutes | Cooking time: 25 minutes | Serves: 2

KEEP IT IN
THE
FAMILY

PHILPS BAKERY IS ACTUALLY KNOWN TO ALL AS PHILPS PASTIES, SINCE THE TRADITIONAL CORNISH FAVOURITE IS THE MAINSTAY OF THIS FAMILY-RUN BUSINESS THAT HAS BEEN THRIVING SINCE 1958.

Some things haven't changed since Philps Bakery was established over six decades ago, like the original pasty recipe and the production site and shop in Hayle, but its popularity has only grown over the years. It all began with Sammy Philp, a grocer who started to sell a few pasties from his shop during the 1950s, and then joined forces with his cousin Everett, a baker.

Thanks to top quality ingredients – Sammy certainly knew his onions, having worked in the industry from the age of 15 – and Everett's serious pastry making skills, the pasties were soon the talk of the county. Although Sammy was still working six days a week at 90 years old, he had technically passed the business on to his sons, Neil and Paul, and his son-in-law, David, in the 1980s. Today it's in the hands of eight Philp's family members, the third generation of pasty-makers and a hard-working bunch passionate about keeping the Philps Bakery ethos alive.

Cousins Lauren, Sam, Stephanie, Gregory, Nina, Freya, Hollie and George all have different roles within the company but work together as one unit. They employ over 100 staff, including many other local families, who crimp, fill and season the pasties completely by hand. These pasties – along with rolls, baps, cakes and bakes – are freshly made every day to be delivered and baked at the seven shops across Cornwall.

Despite their great success, it's important to the Philp family that further expansion is never undertaken if it means compromising on quality. The high grade of the produce used in every product means that going wholesale wouldn't be financially viable, something the company is actually very proud of. Davidstow mature cheddar, beef skirt from a nearby abattoir, bread-grade flour, vegetables grown within a five mile radius of the main shop…this is very much a homemade product on a county-wide scale, true to Cornish tradition and family values.

Luckily for those of us outside Cornwall, Philps' pasties are actually available across the UK delivered by post! The box of your chosen pasties will be made the same day they are sent out, and delivered the next day in time for lunch. From one grocer's shop in Cornwall to fans across the isle and even overseas, the Philps Bakery story has family at heart and continues to flourish.

TRADITIONAL
STEAK PASTY

*The Cornish pasty is regarded as the national dish of Cornwall. Our 'traditional'
Cornish pasty is always made with shortcrust pastry and locally sourced skirt
steak. Even our vegetables are grown within 5 miles of our bakeries, ensuring we
give people the true taste of Cornwall!*

FOR THE SHORTCRUST PASTRY

1kg plain flour
250g solid vegetable fat (we use Stork)
250g lard
Good pinch of salt
350ml cold water

FOR THE FILLING

4 large potatoes, peeled and diced
1 large onion, peeled and diced
½ a swede, peeled and diced
Salt and pepper
560g skirt steak, seasoned
Knob of butter

TO GLAZE

1 beaten egg, diluted with a splash of water

Sieve the flour into a large mixing bowl and cube the vegetable fat and lard. Add them to the flour with a good pinch of salt and rub together to a crumb consistency. Add the cold water and mix until combined; all the water should have been absorbed. Cover and leave to rest in the fridge for 20 to 30 minutes.

Baker's tip: The pastry can be made the day before and placed in the fridge to ensure it is well rested and pliable.

While the pastry is resting, prepare the filling. Mix the peeled and diced vegetables together and season with salt and pepper to taste.

Preheat the oven to 180°c. Remove the pastry from fridge and divide into eight equal balls. On a floured surface with a rolling pin, roll each ball into a dinner plate-sized round about 7-10mm thick. Divide the vegetable mixture equally between each pastry round and add 70g of seasoned skirt steak to each one. Sprinkle with a little flour and add a knob of butter, then fold the pastry round in half carefully, ensuring the filling remains inside, and pinch together to seal.

Your pasty should now be in the traditional 'D' shape. Starting from one end of the pasty, begin to crimp the sealed edge by twisting and pinching to create a 'rope' effect. Once you reach the end, fold the remaining twist over itself with a firm pinch to prevent your crimp unravelling.

Line a baking tray with silicone paper (not greaseproof) and place your pasties on it, leaving space between each one. Brush with the egg glaze and, with a sharp knife, create a steam hole in the centre of each pasty.

Place in a preheated oven for approximately 50 minutes. Check and turn the tray halfway through cooking. Bake until golden and piping hot!

Preparation time: approx. 45 minutes | Cooking time: approx. 50-60 minutes | Makes: 8

VEGETABLE
VEGAN PASTY

*It is the flaky pastry in this recipe that sets this pasty aside from the more
traditional shortcrust variety. It is often compared to puff pastry but includes the
important process of leaving chunks of fat visible throughout, that when baked
create crispy golden flakes.*

FOR THE FLAKY PASTRY

1kg plain flour
455g solid vegetable fat (we use Stork)
Good pinch of salt
570ml cold water

FOR THE FILLING

4 large potatoes, peeled and diced
1 large onion, peeled and diced
½ a swede, peeled and diced
Salt and pepper
Knob of vegetable fat or butter

TO GLAZE

*1 beaten egg, with a splash of water
or alternatively use a splash of soya milk*

Sieve the flour into a large mixing bowl and cut the vegetable fat into 1cm cubes. Add half the fat and a good pinch of salt to the flour, then rub together to a crumb consistency. Add the water and mix until combined and all water has been absorbed. Add the remaining fat and fold into the dough for 2 minutes (leaving chunks of fat visible throughout the pastry) then cover and leave to rest in the fridge for 20 to 30 minutes.

While the pastry is resting, prepare the filling. Mix the vegetables together and season with salt and pepper to taste.

Preheat the oven to 180°c. Remove the pastry from the fridge and divide into eight equal balls. On a floured surface with a rolling pin, roll each ball into a dinner plate-sized round about 7-10mm thick. Divide the vegetable mixture equally between each pastry round and add a knob of vegetable fat or butter to each. At this point, any other filling can be added for non-vegans such as 30g of strong grated cheddar.

Fold the pastry round in half carefully, ensuring the filling remains inside, and pinch together to seal. Your pasty should now be in the traditional 'D' shape. Starting from one end of the pasty, begin to crimp the sealed edge by twisting and pinching to create a 'rope' effect. Once you reach the end, fold the remaining twist over itself with a firm pinch to prevent your crimp unravelling.

Line a baking tray with silicone paper (not greaseproof) and place your pasties on it, leaving space between each one. Brush with your choice of glaze and create a steam hole with a sharp knife in the centre of each pasty.

Place in the preheated oven for approximately 50 minutes. Check and turn the tray halfway through cooking. Your pasties should be golden, crisp and piping hot!

Baker's tip: is eight pasties too many for your family in one go? Pop them in your freezer, individually wrapped in cling film, either raw or cooked to enjoy another day.

Preparation time: approx. 45 minutes | Cooking time: approx. 50-60 minutes | Makes: 8

SAFFRON CAKE

Saffron is the world's most expensive spice by weight and is actually more costly than gold. Luckily a little goes a long way! The spice, which is the stigma of the crocus flower, was originally brought to Cornwall by the Romans and was traded for tin and other goods.

½ tsp saffron strands

110ml warm water

210g plain flour

20g caster sugar

Pinch of salt

45g lard

45g butter (or 90g butter if not wanting to use lard)

7g sachet of dry fast action or instant yeast

80g currants

50g sultanas

20g mixed peel

Grease a 1lb loaf tin with butter. In a small bowl, soak the saffron strands in the warm water, leaving for at least 30 minutes until the water cools to room temperature and the colour is a deep orange.

Baker's tip: for a more intense colour, leave the saffron to infuse overnight.

Sieve the flour into a separate larger bowl and add the sugar, salt, lard if using, and butter. Rub everything between your fingertips to form a crumb. Add the yeast and gently mix. Pour over the saffron infused water, including the strands, and mix to a soft dough.

Turn out the dough onto a lightly floured surface and add the currants, sultanas and mixed peel. Gently knead through for about 15 minutes until evenly mixed. Leave the dough to rest for 15 minutes covered with a tea towel. After the first prove, mould the dough into a baton to fit into the loaf tin and transfer into the tin. Cover with a damp tea towel and leave in a warm place for 30 to 45 minutes or until risen, but not above the top of the tin.

Preheat the oven to 160°c and when up to temperature, place the proved loaf in the centre of the oven and bake for 45 to 60 minutes, or until golden brown.

Remove from the oven and leave in the tin. When cooled, turn the loaf out and slice. Serve with clotted cream or butter.

Preparation time: approx. 1 hour 30 minutes | Cooking time: 45-60 minutes | Serves: 4

HEAVY
'HEVVA' CAKE

Heavy or 'hevva' cake as it was formally known, originates from Cornwall's pilchard industry. 'Huers' (clifftop lookouts) would call 'hevva' to the fishermen below to guide them towards the shoals of pilchards. Their reward was freshly made hevva cake. The criss-cross scoring represented the pilchard nets of the Cornish fishermen.

225g plain flour

Pinch of salt

½ tsp cinnamon

2 level tsp baking powder

80g caster sugar (plus extra for dusting)

55g lard or vegetable shortening (we use Trex)

55g vegetable fat for baking (we use Stork)

55g currants

55g sultanas

4 tbsp water

3 tbsp milk (or soya milk)

Preheat the oven to 180°c. Mix the flour, salt, cinnamon, baking powder, and sugar together in a bowl. Cube the lard or vegetable shortening and the vegetable fat. Add the lard or shortening and vegetable fat to the bowl and rub in with your fingertips until the mixture resembles breadcrumbs. Add the currants and sultanas and mix through. Add the water and bring together with your hands until just forming dough.

Divide the dough into two equal portions. Place on a baking sheet and gently press down to form rounds about 3cm deep, leaving enough space between them to avoid contact during baking.

Score three lines across the top of the cake in one direction and three in another, creating a criss-cross pattern. Glaze each cake with your choice of milk. Sprinkle with sugar and place in the preheated oven to bake for 20 to 25 minutes until golden brown.

Once removed from the oven, sprinkle with more sugar and serve.

Preparation time: 15-20 minutes | Cooking time: 20-25 minutes | Serves: 8 (makes 2 large cakes)

SCONES

A West Country treat, scones are the perfect accompaniment to an afternoon cup of tea. The traditional Cornish way to serve them is to slice the scone in half and spread a layer of jam on first then add a big dollop of Cornish clotted cream on top.

225g self-raising flour

Pinch of salt

2½g bicarbonate of soda

2½g cream of tartar

55g butter, cubed

25g caster sugar

140ml milk

1 egg, beaten

Preheat the oven to 200°c. Mix the flour, salt, bicarbonate of soda and cream of tartar together in a bowl. Add the butter to the dry ingredients and rub together to form a fine crumb. Stir in the sugar with a metal spoon. Make a well in the centre and pour in the milk, then bring together using the spoon until a dough is formed.

Turn out onto a lightly floured surface and roll out gently to a thickness of 1½-2cm. Using a 5cm cutter, press out as many rounds as possible. Bring the remaining dough together gently and repeat the process until all the dough has been used.

Place the scones on a silicone-lined baking tray and brush the tops lightly with the beaten egg. Place into the oven and bake for 10 to 15 minutes until risen and golden.

Baker's tip: for a more indulgent treat, add 30g of sultanas or currants to the dough after the sugar, and serve the scones warm with a layer of strawberry jam and lashings of Cornish clotted cream.

Preparation time: 15-20 minutes | Baking time: 10-15 minutes | Makes: 12-14

SHAKE A

TAIL FEATHER

THIS RENOWNED CORNISH DESTINATION IS A 16TH CENTURY COACHING INN TURNED CONTEMPORARY PUB, COMBINING LUXURY WITH HISTORIC BEAUTY AND A FRESH APPROACH TO COUNTRYSIDE DINING.

The Plume of Feathers stands at a crossroads, which in years gone by would connect the four corners of Cornwall via the roads that dissected the county. This ingrained status as a meeting place carries through into the ethos of the business today, which is family-run with care and dedication. Pete and Jacqui Fair, along with their son Daniel, own The Plume as well as the coastal retreat Lewinnick Lodge. These Cornish gems are distinct in personality but united by their focus on the customer to make sure every visit turns into a great experience that people want to return for.

Nat Tallents, the new chef patron who moved over from her previous role as executive chef to both venues, shares this responsibility where food is concerned. The Plume's menus are designed to be a little bit special as well as honest and affordable, adding a touch of refinement to the pub classics that everybody knows and loves. "It's about using great ingredients, keeping it simple, and celebrating Cornish heritage," says Dan.

Continuing to evolve their plow-to-plate approach to food has meant using not only locally sourced but homegrown produce in signature dishes. The kitchen garden and beehives are just a starting point, soon to be joined by polytunnels for growing vegetables and salads, and chickens. They use a fantastic local wine supplier, also family-run, to complement the food and of course keep a good range of West Country real ales behind the bar, both of which go down nicely at the weddings the pub is now licensed to hold.

For more casual diners, there's breakfast in the conservatory, lunch in the beer garden, or dinner by the fire to enjoy. A true country pub atmosphere – warm, friendly and welcoming – pervades the venue, including its 20 secluded bedrooms for overnight stays. Through the courtyard under original stone arches, former stables, hen houses and hay lofts have been converted into comfortable accommodation. The rustic design but commitment to quality runs throughout, keeping unique features like the covered natural spring well in the pub's floor, which creates a centrepiece in the pub just as The Plume has once again become a centrepiece within the village.

PLATE OF CORNISH LAMB

"This dish encompasses three different cuts of lamb, utilising the neck and breast along with the prime lamb loin. I love slow braising as it really brings out the flavour of these lesser-used cuts." – Nat Tallents, head chef.

1kg lamb neck

20g thyme

3 cloves of garlic

1 onion

2 tbsp garlic purée

2 tbsp chopped thyme leaves

1 lamb breast

500g lamb loin

Pinch of salt and pepper

2 tbsp rapeseed oil, for frying

FOR THE DAUPHINOISE

8 large potatoes, peeled

500ml cream

2 tbsp garlic purée

25g thyme

FOR THE CARROT PURÉE

500g carrots

1 tbsp fennel seeds

50g butter

10g thyme

FOR THE SAUCE

100ml red wine

2 tbsp redcurrant jelly

2 tbsp tomato purée

10g thyme

FOR THE LAMB

Place the lamb neck in a deep roasting dish with the thyme, garlic, onion and enough water to cover. Cook at 160°c for 2 hours 30 minutes until tender. Reserve the braising liquor for the sauce and allow the lamb to cool slightly. Pick all the meat into a bowl, season and then use cling film to roll the picked meat into a tight log. Refrigerate until needed.

Spread the garlic purée, chopped thyme and seasoning over the lamb breast, roll up tightly, cling film tightly then wrap in foil. Cook with the lamb neck for 2 hours 30 minutes on a tray with a good edge as a lot of fat will be released. Allow to cool and then remove the film and foil. Slice into pieces.

Do this when the lamb neck, lamb breast and dauphinoise potatoes are ready and just reheating before you serve the dish. Trim the lamb loin and season, then pan fry all over until golden. Finish in the oven for 5 minutes, allow to rest and then serve.

FOR THE DAUPHINOISE

Peel the potatoes and slice using a mandoline, then layer them up in a deep dish. Heat the cream with the garlic, thyme and seasoning then pour over the potatoes. Cook the dauphinoise at 160°c for around 1 hour 30 minutes. Best made the night before and chilled in the fridge with a slight weight on top, as then it can be portioned much more easily.

FOR THE CARROT PURÉE

Peel and slice the carrots, then sauté them in a pan with the fennel seeds. Add just enough water to cover the carrots, butter and thyme. When the carrots are soft, blitz them in a blender until smooth, adding more butter if the purée feels grainy. Season to taste with salt and pepper.

FOR THE SAUCE

Add the lamb neck sauce to a pan with the red wine, redcurrant jelly, tomato purée and thyme. Boil and reduce to a glossy consistency then pass through a sieve if preferred.

TO SERVE

Place a slice of lamb neck, lamb breast and dauphinoise per person in the oven to reheat. Spoon some carrot purée onto the plate. Add the three cuts of lamb and potato, drizzle with the sauce and serve to impressed guests!

Preparation time: 35 minutes | Cooking time: 2 hours 30 minutes | Serves: 8

RHUBARB
AND CUSTARD

"This take on my favourite flavour combination brings together smooth egg custard, tart rhubarb and biscuit crumb."

FOR THE PASTRY

250g plain flour

100g icing sugar

Pinch of salt

100g butter, slightly softened

3 eggs

FOR THE EGG CUSTARD

250ml double cream

250ml milk

1 vanilla pod

8 egg yolks

100g caster sugar

FOR THE RHUBARB COMPOTE

100g forced rhubarb

50g sugar

2 tbsp water

1 tsp lemon juice

FOR THE RHUBARB CRISPS

1 stick of rhubarb

TO SERVE

Your favourite ice cream

50g ginger biscuits

FOR THE PASTRY

Preheat the oven to 180°c or 160°c fan.

Put all the dry ingredients in a bowl then rub in the softened butter with your fingertips. Make a well in the middle of the mix and add two of the eggs, working them into the dough until it comes together. Knead the dough gently on a floured surface until smooth. Cover with cling film and chill for 30 minutes before use.

On a lightly floured surface, roll the pastry out and use it to line a 20cm tart tin, leaving 2cm of pastry hanging over the edge. Chill for another 30 minutes. Place paper and baking beans over the pastry and blind bake for 20 minutes, then remove the baking beans and paper and bake for a further 8 minutes. Beat the remaining egg and egg wash the baked tart case and set aside. Drop the oven temperature to 140°c or 120°c fan.

FOR THE EGG CUSTARD

Bring the cream, milk and vanilla to the boil in a pan. Beat the egg yolks with the sugar until pale. Pour the hot milk mixture over the eggs, beating as you go. Strain the custard into a jug, allow it to settle then skim off the froth.

Place the tart case on a tray in the oven then pour the egg mixture into the tart, as full as you can possibly get it, and carefully slide back on the oven shelf. Bake for 40 minutes or until just set with the slightest wobble in the very centre.

Grate over some fresh nutmeg and trim off the excess pastry. Cut into 12 slices to serve.

FOR THE RHUBARB COMPOTE

You can make this while the tart is baking. Cut the rhubarb roughly into cubes then add to a pan with the sugar, water and lemon juice. Cook gently until soft.

FOR THE RHUBARB CRISPS

Slice the rhubarb super thin with a sharp knife. Lay the pieces on a baking sheet and bake in a low oven at 90°c until crisp, or use a dehydrator set at 55°c for 12 hours.

TO SERVE

Place a slice of tart on the plate, add a spoonful of rhubarb compote, scatter a few rhubarb crisps on top and serve with a scoop of ice cream. I use rhubarb ice cream from Callestick Farm. Crumble some ginger biscuits on the plate to add a bit of crunch.

Preparation time: 30 minutes | Cooking time: 1 hour 30 minutes | Serves: 12

CLOSER
TO
NATURE

REAL ALE AND REAL FOOD: POLGOOTH INN HAS THE BEST OF BOTH
WORLDS AND REVELS IN CORNWALL'S FINEST PRODUCE.

Despite being so close to the coast, Polgooth Inn is a proper Cornish country pub, set in seven acres of land with a kitchen garden, making the most of the area's bounty with food and drink that's as fresh and local as it gets. The building itself can lay claim to over 400 years of history, evident in the beautiful interiors that combine original features with cosy but contemporary style. The inn was used by tin miners during the 18th century and apparently shared by all manner of animals over the years! These days, the animals are outside the pub's four walls but not too far away, thanks to the focus on local produce and seasonal food when it comes to the Polgooth's menu.

Traditional classics and modern dishes with a little twist are served all day at the inn, and breakfast is available on a Friday and Saturday morning. The 'Polgooth Pride' is a regularly changing special that might take inspiration from any cuisine, and there are two gardeners and an experienced butcher on site, so lots of the produce used at Polgooth Inn is home-grown and prepared in-house. Everything else, from crab in the summer to venison in the winter, is sourced as

locally as possible. Paying attention to seasonality includes growing unusual varieties of fruit and vegetables that the gardeners, who work under senior head chef Jon Moyle, like to experiment with. Heritage tomatoes and carrots in a rainbow of colours, small but tasty cucamelons, super sweet yellow mange tout…as Tanya puts it, "Anything that can be associated with food and drink, we like to get involved with!"

Husband and wife team Alex and Tanya took on the business in 2010 with their two young children, and are committed to the community around them as well as food and drink that's "up a notch from the norm" in their running of the pub. Their experience in the industry and, more importantly, a love for what they do won the pair Licensee of the Year in the British Institute of Inn-Keeping 2018 awards. They are always looking for new ways to evolve and update the business, as long as Cornish produce stays firmly centre stage. They are currently expanding into beekeeping to produce their own honey, and love to add new and exciting developments to their livelihood whenever the opportunity arises!

HOUSE SMOKED MACKEREL

This is a dish inspired by all that's fresh and locally available to us at Polgooth Inn.
A classic combination of rich oily fish, which is line-caught and smoked in house,
with a light salad accompaniment of radishes, fennel and citrus, much of which is
grown in our kitchen garden.

2 mackerel fillets

28g salt

Pinch of white pepper

5g fresh dill

Oak wood chips, for smoking

2 radishes

1 fennel bulb

1 stick of rhubarb

1 red chilli (cayenne)

¼ of a cucumber

5ml cider vinegar

Fresh micro coriander, for garnish

Place the mackerel fillets on a tray and sprinkle them evenly with the salt, pepper and dill. Cover and leave for 15 minutes to draw out the excess moisture from the fillets. Rinse off the excess salt under cold water and pat dry. Place on a wire rack. Light the wood chips in a deep roasting tray and when they are fully smoking, place the rack with the fish over the wood chips. Cover tightly with foil and leave for 5 minutes to smoke.

Meanwhile, thinly slice the radishes, fennel, rhubarb, red chilli and cucumber. Place it all into a bowl and toss with the cider vinegar, then season with a pinch of salt and pepper. Transfer the smoked mackerel fillets to a baking tray, skin side up, and place under a hot grill. If you have a blow torch, use that instead; you are looking to char the skin without cooking the fillet.

TO SERVE

Arrange a small handful of the pickled vegetable mix in the centre of the plate. Gently place the mackerel fillets on top and garnish with a sprinkle of fresh micro coriander. Sit back and enjoy!

Preparation time: 15-20 minutes | Cooking time: 5 minutes, plus 5 minutes smoking | Serves: 2

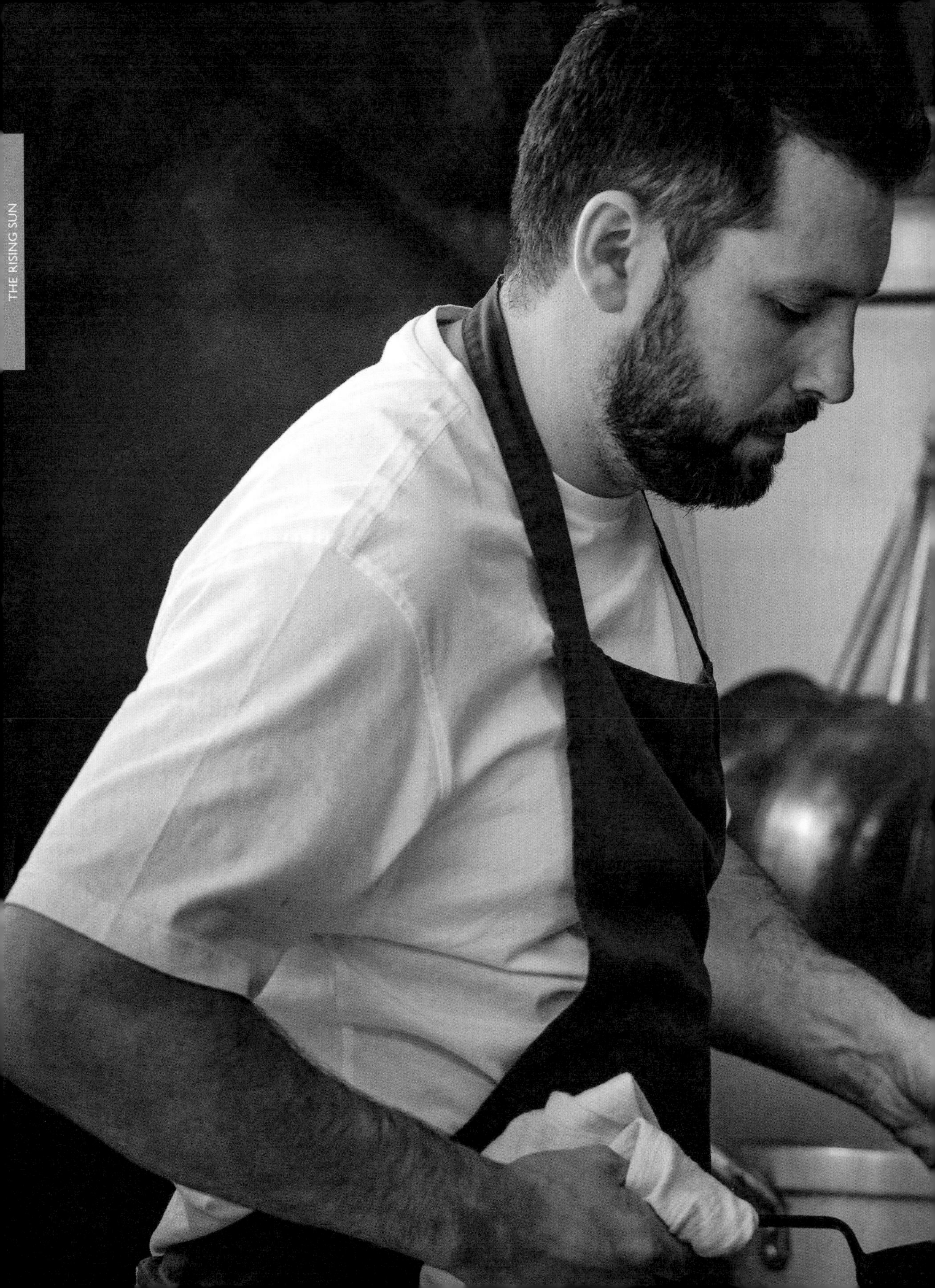

A RAY OF
CORNISH
SUNSHINE

BRINGING ELEMENTS OF FINE DINING TO A RELAXED CORNISH PUB HAS
SET THE RISING SUN ON AN UPWARD TREND IN TRURO.

The Rising Sun had been closed for a year when Tom and Katie came to its rescue in 2014. They undertook a full refit of the venue, and remade the business in their own image of everything a warm, welcoming Cornish pub should be, with top notch food and drink to boot. As a chef by trade, Tom brought his classical style of cooking and the ethos of a Michelin-starred kitchen to his first venture. By applying this approach to a casual setting, the couple could create a true village pub feel while maintaining exacting standards that makes each eating and drinking experience great quality and, above all, enjoyable.

Their attention to detail runs through every aspect of the business, and all products are hand-picked including coffee roasted nearby and the first single-estate English tea in the country. Local and seasonal ingredients form the backbone of everything, and there's no set menu so that dishes can evolve organically. The Rising Sun works very closely with suppliers – someone will be on the phones every morning finding out what's available – and is licensed to buy fish and seafood directly from the boats that land it. Provenance and traceability form a crucial part of Tom and Katie's ethos when

it comes to food and drink, and they pride themselves on making the vast majority in-house, from bread to ice cream.

"It's a slice of us," says Tom about the venture, which has been growing in success due in significant part, he thinks, to The Rising Sun's individuality. He and Katie are very hands-on when it comes to running the pub from a kitchen and front of house point of view; making sure everyone's on the same page means customers can enjoy the whole experience without a hitch. Most of the team have been working together for a long time, and their attitude of putting people first is intrinsic to the friendly atmosphere at The Rising Sun.

Customers have really taken to it and embraced Tom and Katie's vision, within Truro's community as well as seasonal visitors. There is something for everyone on the menu, whether you fancy proper fish and chips or a trio of lamb, and because of the owners' passion and drive to continually move the business forward it's never merely standing still. From regional accolades to Food Magazine's 'Best Foodie Pub' award in 2019, The Rising Sun is, like its namesake, always on the up!

A TASTE
OF SUMMER

This is a great recipe to have on hand as it's so versatile. The ice cream and meringues can be made in advance, you can change the fruit with the seasons and add elements of it, such as the beignets, to other desserts or enjoy them as an afternoon tea treat.

FOR THE ICE CREAM BASE

300ml milk

300ml double cream

1 tsp vanilla extract

6 egg yolks

300g caster sugar

FOR THE LEMON CURD

3 lemons

120g caster sugar

2 eggs

1 egg yolk

175g butter, diced

FOR THE MINI MERINGUES

2 egg whites

120g caster sugar

FOR THE BEIGNETS

125ml water

50g unsalted butter

Small pinch of salt

75g plain flour, sifted

2 eggs

½ tsp ground cinnamon

200g caster sugar

TO SERVE

1 punnet of strawberries

1 punnet of raspberries

1 punnet of blackberries

Sprig of lemon balm cress

FOR THE LEMON CURD ICE CREAM

To make the ice cream base, combine the milk, cream and vanilla extract in a saucepan and bring to the boil. In a separate saucepan, beat the egg yolks and caster sugar together. Pour the milk mixture over the creamed yolks, continually mixing to combine everything. Return the mixture to a low heat, continually stirring until it thickens enough to coat the back of a wooden spoon. Take off the heat and allow to cool, then place in an ice cream machine to churn.

To make the lemon curd, first zest and juice the lemons. Combine the caster sugar, eggs, egg yolk, zest and juice in a pan then bring to the boil, continually stirring until the mixture reaches a thick consistency. Take off the heat and whisk in the butter then allow to cool to room temperature. When the ice cream base has churned, gently fold in the lemon curd to create a ripple effect and place in the freezer.

FOR THE MINI MERINGUES

Whip the egg whites while gradually adding the sugar to create stiff peaks. Using a piping bag, pipe mini meringue shapes onto parchment paper (think baby gems!). Put in a warm place to dry.

FOR THE BEIGNETS

Bring the water, butter and salt to the boil then remove from the heat and add the flour in one go. Stir immediately until the flour and liquid are evenly combined. Return to the heat and beat continuously for 3 minutes. Transfer to an electric mixer, beat for 2 minutes then thoroughly incorporate one egg for 1 minute before adding the next. The mixture should now be smooth and glossy. Transfer to a piping bag and refrigerate.

Preheat a deep fat fryer or pan of oil to 180°c. Use scissors to snip evenly sized pieces of the beignet mixture into the fryer as you squeeze it out of the piping bag. Continually rotate and baste the beignets with hot oil until golden brown, then transfer from the fryer to a cooling rack. Combine the cinnamon and sugar, then roll the cooled beignets in the mixture.

TO SERVE

Place a scoop of the lemon curd ice cream in the centre of a large bowl. Prepare the fresh fruit and delicately place the berries, mini meringues and beignets around and on the ice cream, then garnish with lemon balm and serve.

Preparation time: 30 minutes | Cooking time: 2 hours | Serves: 6

ALL

FIRED
UP

CULINARY DUO SCOTT AND BABS PROVIDE A UNIQUE DINING
EXPERIENCE WITH THEIR WOOD-FIRED OVENS AND PARTY ATMOSPHERE,
TUCKED AWAY IN A PEACEFUL CORNISH VALLEY.

Retorrick Mill is home to many things including a working farm, self-catering accommodation, wedding venue and more, but it's the restaurant at the heart of it all where Scott and Babs keep everyone fed and very happy, and the owner Wilf runs his super cosy bar. Scott and Babs originally intended to travel with their catering business, but their first pop up at their friend Wilf's venue – the former stables at Retorrick Mill – went down so well that they've had to stick around!

The open kitchen uses wood-fired ovens, smoking barrels and spit roasts to create a menu that changes every day and is born out of seasonal and local produce. From sit down meals to all-out Sunday banquets, the food offering is eclectic and developed according to events held at the venue. Live music pairs with pizza and dancing on the tables goes hand in hand with plenty of good rum for wild Saturday nights, and the annual May festival brings everyone out to the countryside for food and fun.

Scott and Babs want visitors to enjoy the lifestyle at Retorrick Mill as much as they do, along with their team who have all worked together for years. Word of mouth is how news of their food and location get around Cornwall and the locals certainly don't want to give up the secret, as bookings fill up way in advance and the summer months especially are always jam-packed.

The pair do get to travel when the venue closes for a couple of months over winter, picking up ideas for their food along the way. "Our inspiration is based on what's around us at the time," says Scott. The same goes for the décor of the barn, which used to mean everyone was eating alongside old bits of farm machinery and hay bales, but now it's peppered with tables made from trees grown in the surrounding acres. Nothing matches, and there are no airs or graces to speak of which is all part of the rustic charm.

Retorrick Mill is only a mile from Magwan Porth beach and set amidst beautiful countryside. Coupled with the quirky vibe and laid-back approach to good Cornish fun, the venue has everything going for it, not least the smoky flavours and inventive eats from the incomparable Scott and Babs!

JANNER TURBOT, PORTHILLY CLAMS
AND CORNISH ASPARAGUS

*We consider turbot to be the 'pig's head' of the sea with its gelatinous meaty flesh, the
perfect accompaniment to which is juicy spring clams and local asparagus.*

I tsp yellow mustard seeds

I tsp brown mustard seeds

Cider vinegar

6-8lb (2.7-3.6kg) whole turbot

I lemon, sliced

I tbsp fennel seeds, ground

Olive oil

Sea salt

100g butter

Bunch of asparagus

1kg Porthilly clams

4 bay leaves

Fresh parsley

Light the wood-fired oven around 2 hours prior to cooking. Bring up to 400°c to
ensure you are cooking on a dropping temperature.

Soak the mustard seeds in cider vinegar until soft. Wash and dry the turbot using
paper towel. Trim around the head and on the inside of the fins. Score the skin.
Line a tray with greaseproof paper and oil it well, then place the fish in the centre.
Place the sliced lemon, ground fennel seeds, a drizzle of oil, a pinch of salt and the
butter on the topside of the fish.

Put the tray in the preheated oven and cook for 20 minutes. Baste the fish with
the juices while cooking to keep it moist. The fish is cooked when white juices are
released and the meat is coming away from the bone.

Leave the fish to rest for 10 minutes while you steam the asparagus for 30 seconds
and cook the clams in a saucepan with the bay leaves, soaked mustard seeds and a
splash of water. Cook until all the clams are fully open.

Remove the upper layer of skin from the fish then serve everything together on the
tray. Finish with a scattering of chopped parsley and tuck in.

Preparation time: approx. 30 minutes | Cooking time: 30 minutes (at 300°c in a wood-fired oven) | Serves: 4 hungry people

A MATCH MADE IN

SEASIDE
HEAVEN

HANDCRAFTED GINS AND LIQUEURS GO HAND-IN-HAND WITH A VIBRANT TAPAS MENU AT SILCO SEAROOM IN THE BEAUTIFUL CORNISH TOWN OF ST IVES.

The Thompson family are proprietors of not one but two thriving businesses in the popular Cornish town of St Ives, from which they draw inspiration for their unique food and drink. The Searoom was established in 2014 after mum Tamsin began cooking at the tearoom, as it was then, a couple of days a week. Her sons – Tim, Greg and Bertie – also came on board, and gradually they transformed the business into a contemporary bar and restaurant complete with retail space with the help of dad Pete who, handily, is a carpenter by trade and made the venture a true family affair.

This set-up is a perfect shop window for the gins and liqueurs created by the St Ives Liquor Company (or SILCo) which sprung from the Searoom's success. The Thompson brothers launched their new venture in 2017 having begun with a single cold compound gin which they made behind the bar. Two flavoured gins followed, and then a limoncello and a pompelmocello (grapefruit flavoured liqueur) joined the line up on the back of the gins' immense popularity. SILCo drinks are now supplied to more than a hundred businesses across Cornwall and far beyond. "It's been a totally unexpected but brilliant new aspect of the business," says Tim.

The bar and restaurant, now known as SILCo Searoom, doesn't take bookings, allowing everyone from locals in the off-season to returning holidaymakers to wander in and soak up the relaxed but bubbly atmosphere at any time. With equal emphasis placed on the food and drink, plus SILCo products and merchandise, everyone from families to couples can stay as long as they like, eat whatever they like from the eclectic tapas menu, and enjoy tip-top views over the beach.

'You get out what you put in' is the family motto when it comes to ingredients, so they forage for gin botanicals, champion locally caught fish and seafood and always use seasonal vegetables. Influences range from British, Mediterranean, Asian and Spanish courtesy of the head chef, who along with his team cooks all the food fresh to order. Over the last few years multiple gold Good Food awards have come their way, and the Thompsons are keen to build on the early success of SILCo too by holding more tasting events, expanding the shop and creating more products – gin is just the start!

GRILLED CORNISH MACKEREL WITH TOMATO SALAD AND SALSA VERDE

Serve up summertime the SILCo Searoom way. Surprisingly simple and fantastically fresh, this dish has stood the test of time on our ever-changing menu. With a SILCo G&T in hand and the sun shining, this one takes some beating.

4 thick slices of local sourdough bread

8 Cornish mackerel fillets

FOR THE TOMATO SALAD

700g English mixed colour heritage tomatoes

1 small red onion

40g cornichons

25g baby capers

30g caster sugar

1 tbsp Cornish sea salt

60ml red wine vinegar

FOR THE SALSA VERDE

1 tsp baby capers

1 clove of garlic

3 tbsp chopped parsley

4 tbsp extra-virgin olive oil

½ a lemon, zested and juiced

Cornish sea salt, to taste

TO SERVE

Small bunch of mixed fresh herbs (for example: parsley, basil, coriander)

Extra-virgin olive oil

FOR THE TOMATO SALAD

Chop the tomatoes into bite-size chunks and place in a large bowl. Peel and very finely slice the red onion into half-moons. Slice the cornichons lengthways and add to the bowl. Add the capers. Sprinkle over the sugar and sea salt then add the vinegar. Stir gently and then leave aside to marinate for about 30 minutes. After this time, give them another stir and then drain them through a large sieve, discarding the liquid.

FOR THE SALSA VERDE

While the tomatoes marinate, make the salsa verde. Finely chop the capers. Crush the garlic and combine with the parsley and capers in a bowl. Add the olive oil, lemon zest and a squeeze or two of lemon juice. Mix well, season with salt and taste.

Toast the sourdough on a hot griddle pan after drizzling olive oil on both sides and rubbing in gently. Turn when it has good colour on one side to toast the other.

While the bread is toasting, place the mackerel fillets on a baking tray. Drizzle over a little olive oil and season with sea salt. Place the fillets under a hot grill, skin side up. Grill for 5 minutes or until the fish is just cooked through and flaky.

TO SERVE

Add the roughly chopped mixed herbs to the drained tomatoes and drizzle with olive oil. Place the toasted sourdough slices on four plates and pile the tomato salad onto each one. Top with the mackerel fillets and drizzle the salsa verde over and around the fish and bread. Cornish, fresh, healthy and delicious!

Preparation time: 20 minutes, plus 30 minutes marinating | Cooking time: 10 minutes | Serves: 4

A COMMUNITY
FULL
OF FLAVOUR

MAKING LOCAL PRODUCE AVAILABLE TO THE PEOPLE OF ST IVES
IS THE MISSION STATEMENT OF THE TOWN FARMERS' MARKET,
SET UP BY A COMMUNITY GROUP TO BRING FANTASTIC CORNISH
INGREDIENTS TOGETHER.

St Ives Farmers' Market has gone from strength to strength since it was established in 2008 with just six stalls; today over 30 independent traders fill the town's Guildhall with local produce every Thursday between 9:30am and 2pm all year round. The enterprise was dreamt up by a community group based in St Ives who wanted to provide a local shopping facility that made quality produce grown, reared, cured, crafted, distilled and brewed within 30 miles of St Ives readily available.

This primary aim is supplemented by a few extra touches that give the venue a true community feel. Buskers play live music in a designated space within the hall, charity stalls raise money for good causes, and there is a café serving food made with local produce, from hot drinks to light lunches. All of this attention to detail makes visiting the market an experience rather than just a shopping trip, which is an important part of the founding group's ethos.

"The ability for shoppers to actually speak with stall holders about the food or crafts they sell – provenance, how the animals have been reared and looked after, using their ingredients in cooking – is something we really value about farmers' markets," says Tim, a member of the group. They are now looking towards embracing the plastic-free movement, something that is close to Cornish hearts, especially in St Ives with such proximity to and understanding of the ocean's welfare.

This strong sense of what a market should be, and the connection to the town and surrounding area, has contributed to the venture's development and popularity over the years. Taste of the West awarded it Best Farmer's Market in the Southwest two years running: no surprise when you see the colourful range of food and more on offer. Stalls laden with organic vegetables, fresh fish and seafood, pork and beef, baked goods both savoury and sweet, preserves, and even gins made by the very local St Ives Liquor Company (SILCo) populate the hall on a weekly basis. From international flavours to vegan and vegetarian delights, everything you need for a week's delicious home-grown meals (plus lunch and a treat for the day!) can be found and enjoyed at St Ives Farmers' Market.

ST IVES HAKECAKES WITH ORANGE AND WATERCRESS SAUCE

The folk of St Ives are traditionally referred to as 'hakes' after the glorious fish that swim in our waters. This recipe uses hake in these fishcakes along with other traditional ingredients: potatoes, leeks and cabbage used in Irish Colcannon and Cornish 'Teddy' cake. This collaboration is a celebration of St Patrick and St Piran's Day, complemented by a zesty dipping sauce.

FOR THE FISHCAKES

1 fillet of hake (approx. 200g), washed and scaled

1 lemon, zested and juiced

1 lime, zested and juiced

Sea salt and black pepper

140ml milk

2 floury potatoes, washed and cut into small chunks

Knob of butter

Olive oil

2 cloves of garlic, crushed

2 leeks, washed and finely chopped

150g sweetheart cabbage or kale, washed and finely chopped

1 bunch of parsley, chopped

1 egg, beaten (optional)

2 tbsp oatmeal

2 tbsp polenta

FOR THE SAUCE

285ml milk

1 orange

1 tbsp olive oil

1 bunch of watercress (approx. 150g), chopped

2 tbsp flour

FOR THE FISHCAKES

Coat the fish in the citrus zest and juices, season and place in the fridge overnight to marinate. You don't have to do this, but it does improve the flavour. Transfer the hake to a saucepan, pour over the milk and gently poach for 8 minutes. Drain and keep the liquid for the sauce.

Preheat the oven to 180°c while you boil the potatoes in a pan of slightly salted water until cooked. Drain and place in a large bowl with a knob of butter. Heat a tablespoon of oil in a frying pan, then add the crushed garlic and leeks, followed by the cabbage or kale and parsley. Season with salt and pepper, stir well and sauté until cooked (about 10 minutes). Now you're ready to make the cakes!

Mash the potatoes in the bowl then add the cooked veg. Flake the fish and fold into the mixture. Add the beaten egg if using and check the consistency. It should be moist and creamy but firm enough to shape. Thicken with a little oatmeal if necessary. Mix the oatmeal and polenta together and spread across a tray or chopping board. Shape the mixture into burger-sized cakes before rolling each in the oatmeal and polenta coating. You should get 10 or 12 cakes. Heat two tablespoons of olive oil in the frying pan and gently shallow fry the fishcakes, turning once until golden both sides. Transfer to the oven when cooked to keep warm. These are now ready to serve, or you can use the number required then cool and freeze the rest.

FOR THE SAUCE

Add the liquid left from cooking the fish to the rest of the milk. Zest the orange, juice it, then scoop out the pulp. Add the orange juice to the milk but keep the zest and pulp. You should have about 570ml of liquid, so top up with milk or orange juice if needed. Heat the oil in a pan then add the chopped watercress, orange zest and seasoning. Stir well and cook for 4 minutes before stirring in the flour. Slowly add the milk mixture and keep stirring. Finally add the orange pulp and cook for a further 3 minutes. Check the consistency and taste – the sauce should be smooth, not too thick – and add more seasoning or liquid if required.

TO SERVE

This dish can be served as a starter using one hakecake per portion or mains using two. Place the cakes on a plate with the sauce alongside for dipping. Serve with fresh slices of orange twisted on top of the cakes, a selection of olives and mixed leaf salad. Or, top with a free-range poached egg, a sprinkle of freshly grated Parmesan and steamed purple sprouting broccoli.

Preparation time: 35 minutes, plus overnight marinating (optional) | Cooking time: 50 minutes | Serves: 6

THE
DAILY
SCOOP

RUN BY A SELF-TAUGHT COOK WITH A UNIQUE APPROACH TO HER CRAFT, TALL SHIPS CREAMERY PRODUCES LUXURY HANDMADE CORNISH ICE CREAMS AND SWEET TREATS WITH LOVE IN EVERY SCOOP.

For shop owner and ice cream maker Victoria, her business is her passion as well as her livelihood. She swapped London life for running a guesthouse in Cornwall, where the popularity of her desserts – and ice cream in particular – brought her dream of owning an ice cream shop a little closer to reality. When Victoria found an empty building in Charlestown that she knew would be a perfect fit, she only needed her ideas and her love of making ice cream to get started. After doing up the shop, leasing an ice cream machine and teaching herself the processes, Tall Ships Creamery started to sell sweet treats and has never looked back!

"My secret has always been consistency and perseverance," says Victoria. "I also want my products to be as healthy but as scrumptious as possible, which makes them quite different to a lot of businesses'." Tall Ships' ice cream is made with far less refined sugar because it uses lots of fresh fruit for natural sweetness, alongside top quality ingredients. Local milk and cream are combined with any flavour you can think of – there are over 80 in the full range – but never with air or artificial additives. The motto behind the making is "if you give, you get" which is why Victoria puts only the best into her ice cream, as well as all the other treats created at Tall Ships Creamery. She is also especially considerate of dietary requirements, with dairy-free, gluten-free, vegan and diabetic-friendly options aplenty.

A second shop, just across the road from the first, joined the business to sell freshly baked pies, cakes and signature heart-shaped scones alongside the raw fudge, cold drinks and, of course, the ice cream. The four core flavours of chocolate, vanilla, mint and strawberry are available all year round, while other flavours rotate according to the season and Victoria's imagination! Her pirate-themed names nod to the port town that Tall Ships Creamery calls home, and some of her ice creams will even star in a series of children's books which Victoria plans to publish soon. Her whimsical sense of fun is underpinned by the absolute passion and dedication with which she runs her business. "You're only as good as your team," she points out, "and we're like best friends at Tall Ships so a happy team means great ice cream!"

BELGIAN CHOCOLATE BOOTY BROWNIE WITH VANILLA GOLD ICE CREAM

A celebration of two sweet treats coming together to create the perfect gluten-free pudding. When partnered with my Vanilla Gold Ice Cream, this brownie is heaven. I love to top the whole thing with chopped chocolate, nuts or fresh fruit too.

300g dark chocolate (at least 60% cocoa solids)

175g cold unsalted butter

300g light muscovado sugar

5 eggs

175g gluten-free plain flour

30g cocoa powder

1 litre of Tall Ships Creamery Cornish Vanilla Gold Ice Cream

OPTIONAL TOPPINGS

Chocolate, nuts or fruit of your choice, chopped or crumbled

Gluten-free ice cream cones

Chocolate sauce

Preheat the oven to 200°c. Lightly grease a brownie tin and line with baking parchment.

Put the chocolate in a large heatproof bowl with the butter and place over a pan of gently simmering water, stirring occasionally until melted and smooth. Remove from the heat, stir in the sugar, then allow to cool slightly.

Gradually add the eggs to the chocolate mixture, beating well between additions. Sift the flour and cocoa over the mixture and fold together. The mixture should be thick and glossy. Spoon the mixture into the prepared tin and bake for 15 to 18 minutes or until the top is firm to the touch, but the centre is still slightly sticky when tested with the tip of a knife. You should see cracks appear on the top; this gives the brownie a good crust but a gooey centre. Leave to cool in the tin so it can firm up.

Once cold, remove from the tin and cut the brownies into 10 rectangles. When ready to serve, you can slightly warm each brownie in the microwave for 15 seconds and then top with a scoop of Tall Ships Creamery Vanilla Gold Ice Cream. Add whatever decorative extras you like and enjoy!

Preparation time: 15 minutes | Cooking time: 15-18 minutes | Serves: 10

PUTTING DOWN

NEW ROOTS

THE LITTLE TEAROOM NESTLED WITHIN THE MAGNIFICENT TREWIDDEN GARDEN IS BLOOMING ONCE AGAIN WITH THE HELP OF TWO LOCAL AND DEDICATED CAFÉ OWNERS.

Trewidden Garden is one of the Great Gardens of Cornwall, originally planted in the 19th century by an ancestor of Alverne Bolitho who owns the estate today, which has been in his family since the 1700s. Some of the unique attractions include one of the foremost collections of tree ferns in the northern hemisphere, award-winning camellias, and of course a picturesque tearoom that's something of a hidden gem. This is now in the capable and enthusiastic hands of Dave and Nat who are also the people behind Duke St. Café in Newlyn. The two businesses are less than a few miles apart and similar in style, with plenty of proper food made with Cornish ingredients and a welcoming atmosphere that invites people to return for more than a homemade cake or a spot of light lunch.

The opportunity to run Trewidden Garden's tearoom was offered to Dave and Nat because of the reputation they have built at Duke St Café. The estate approached them back in 2018, feeling that the tearoom would benefit from the same dedication to both the food and feel of the venue. Dave and Nat set about renovating the small space which was originally a potting shed but had been transformed into a lovely little tearoom in a stunning setting. The house and gardens are somewhat off the beaten track, which can provide a quiet escape from it all in the height of Cornwall's tourist season! The project has been a team effort, with staff from Duke St. also working at the tearoom, intrinsically linking the two local ventures.

The plan is to keep improving and investing in the business, with a view to becoming a real destination eatery. Currently the opening times are seasonally led, but the friendly and accessible approach to hospitality is something Dave and Nat have brought with them from Duke St. Café, so they are aiming to welcome people into Trewidden Tearooms all year round soon enough. Sunday roasts will be added to the menu alongside the breakfast, lunch, and homemade cream tea on offer.

"It's a work in progress right now," says Dave, "but this is a small café with big potential so we are looking forward to really getting underway and moving forwards from there."

RASPBERRY, LIME AND PISTACHIO CAKE

This cake is a real summery treat that looks beautiful and even won us best in show at our local spring show!

FOR THE CAKE

400g Stork

400g caster sugar

6 medium eggs

350g self-raising flour

1 tbsp baking powder

60g pistachios, finely chopped in a food processor (save 10g for decorating)

100g raspberries (fresh or frozen)

1 lime, zested and juiced

FOR THE ICING

180g unsalted butter, softened

300g icing sugar

1 lime, zested

TO FINISH

2 tbsp seedless raspberry jam

Fresh raspberries

Lime zest

Whole pistachios

Grease and line two 23cm round cake tins and preheat the oven to 180°c or 170°c fan. Use a hand mixer to combine the Stork and sugar in the bowl until light and creamy. Add two eggs, whisk thoroughly to avoid the mixture separating, then repeat until all the eggs are incorporated. Fold in the flour, baking powder and ground pistachios. If using fresh raspberries, chop half of them and leave the other half whole. If frozen, just use the end of a rolling pin to crush lightly. Stir the raspberries into the cake batter with the lime zest and juice, folding in until combined.

Spoon the mixture evenly between the two prepared tins and smooth down the surfaces. Place the cakes in the preheated oven and check after 20 minutes. If they look firm stick a skewer in the middle; if it comes out clean the cake is done but if it still has a wobble, shut the door and check again in 5 minute intervals until done.

While the cake is baking, mix the softened butter with the icing sugar and lime zest until light and creamy. Once the cakes are completely cold, spread a thin layer of the raspberry jam on one half along with half the icing, then sandwich the two halves together and spread the rest of the icing on top. Decorate however you wish with the fresh raspberries, lime zest and pistachios.

Preparation time: 10 minutes | Cooking time: 25 minutes | Serves: 12-14

RELAXING
ON THE
UPPERDECK

WITH A FAMILY-FRIENDLY WELCOME, AMAZING VIEWS OVER FALMOUTH MARINA AND A MOUTH-WATERING MENU, UPPERDECK IS THE PLACE BRINGING EVERYONE TOGETHER ON CORNWALL'S FAL ESTUARY.

In 2016 UpperDeck came under new ownership, had a complete refurbishment and became a bar and restaurant with something for everyone. It joined a sister business, Castaways in Mylor Harbour, which came under Toby's ownership in 2003 thanks to the former accountant's love of Cornwall which stemmed from childhood holidays in the area. The team today is driven by head chef Antony and front of house manager Emma, who continue to ensure that UpperDeck can be a meeting place for all those holidaying around Falmouth as well as regular customers.

The interior of the venue reflects its marina-side location, with a huge tank of exotic fish and a boat suspended from the ceiling setting the theme. UpperDeck is, as its name might suggest, on the first floor of the building and fronted by large windows stretching up to high ceilings, treating diners to views over the marina in the open, bright and airy space. The layout is designed to make it just as suitable for a breakfast to set you up, a daytime catch up over a hot drink and homemade cake, or an evening meal from the hearty seasonal menu.

Antony's style of cooking is wholesome, hearty and warming. He takes influences from any inspirational cuisines but the focus is pub-style food made with local ingredients, with an elegance and refined approach to preparing and plating coming in for evening dishes. Steaks sourced from West Country farmers, seafood landed in Newlyn and Plymouth and pizzas freshly made to order are mainstays of the menu but options range from vegan plates to Cornish antipasti to suit all tastes. If you're just popping in for a drink, homemade bar snacks will sort out any cravings, and there's a wide selection of wine, ale, cider and gin to cover all bases.

Thanks to the emphasis on UpperDeck's friendly feel, the restaurant is genuinely welcoming for families as well as being a great meeting place for anyone throughout the day. Live music events take place in the venue every month, showcasing local acts and adding to the lively atmosphere of the unique waterside destination.

DUO OF DUCK
WITH POTATO RÖSTI

This dish celebrates the various ways of utilising duck in cooking: a classic year-round dinner. This recipe does require a bit of work, but it will leave your mouth watering and become a firm favourite amongst friends! It has been a staple on our winter menu and is much loved by our head chef, Antony Riley.

FOR THE DUCK LEG BONBON

1 duck leg

Sea salt

Cumin seeds

Duck fat

1 bouquet garni (fresh parsley, bay leaf, thyme)

½ spring onion, finely chopped

Flour

2 eggs, beaten

Breadcrumbs (panko are best)

FOR THE POTATO RÖSTI

3 large potatoes

50g butter

FOR THE ROOT VEG

100g baby carrots

100g baby parsnips

50ml honey

Sprig of sage

TO FINISH

1 duck breast

200ml red wine

2 tbsp redcurrant jelly

FOR THE DUCK LEG BONBON

Rub the duck leg with sea salt and cumin seeds, then leave it to marinate overnight. The next day, rub off the marinade and place the legs into a deep tray. Cover with duck fat, add the bouquet garni, cover the tray and cook in the oven at 130°c for 3 hours 30 minutes, or until soft. Cool for 30 minutes then strip the meat off the duck legs and combine with the chopped spring onion.

Divide the mixture into four and shape into balls with wet hands. Place in the fridge to set for 30 minutes. Roll the balls in flour, dip them into the beaten egg then coat in breadcrumbs. Set aside.

FOR THE POTATO RÖSTI

Place the unpeeled potatoes into a pan of cold water, bring to the boil and cook for 5 minutes. Drain and leave to cool for 30 minutes. Grate the potatoes, add the butter and season to taste. Press the mixture into a small metal ring until firm, or shape by hand. Transfer the rösti into a frying pan, add a splash of oil and fry on a medium to high heat, allowing the rösti to colour on one side. Flip carefully and repeat the process. Finish the rösti in the oven at 180°c for 12 minutes then leave to cool.

FOR THE ROOT VEG

Cook the carrots and parsnips in a pan of boiling seasoned water for 3 minutes, then transfer straight into very cold water. Drain the veg then coat in the honey and sage. Leave to marinate.

TO FINISH

Trim the duck breast and score the skin. Place the breast skin side down into a hot dry pan and leave until the skin is golden. Carefully flip the breast over and place the pan into the oven at 180°c for 6 minutes.

In a separate hot pan, fry the rösti and duck bonbon in two tablespoons of duck fat until lightly coloured all over. Add the marinated carrots and parsnips and place that pan into the oven for 3 minutes.

When the duck has finished cooking, remove from the oven and let it rest for 6 minutes. Meanwhile, use the pan you cooked the duck in to make the sauce. Stir and reduce the red wine and redcurrant jelly in the pan until you have a sauce consistency.

To serve, slice the duck breast down the centre, share everything between two plates and enjoy!

Preparation time: 1 hour 30 minutes, plus marinating overnight | Cooking time: 3 hours 45 minutes | Serves: 2

A WINNING APPROACH

TWO PASSIONATE PUB PATRONS ARE TRANSFORMING THE VICTORY INN BACK INTO THE LOCAL FAVOURITE AND FOODIE DESTINATION IT ONCE WAS, AT THE HEART OF ST MAWES.

The building that houses The Victory Inn dates back to sometime during the 17th century, but it has recently been given a new lease of life by husband and wife team Matt and Jodie. They re-opened the business in 2017 with the aim of bringing the pub up to date without losing touch with its roots.

Having "ear-marked" the opportunity at a stage where he was keen to have full control following success in two rosette kitchens, chef Matt decided the history and connection of the place was too much of a draw to resist. He and Jodie undertook a full refurbishment, supported by the brewery owners, including an entirely new kitchen, at the end of their first year at the helm.

What they did keep though, was the memorabilia – such as photos going decades back – that intrinsically linked the historic inn to the sailing community in St Mawes. "It all has meaning to the locals, and to us now, which is so important as we don't want to exclude the people who live here year-round by not understanding what they want," says Matt.

What they do want to do is exceed expectations, taking the pub food up a notch from what you might be used to. The menu is deceptively simple – the dishes, like gammon with eggs, chips and grilled pineapple, are recognisable and homely – but belies the extra care and attention to detail which goes into each element.

Matt bakes his own bread, makes ice cream in a multitude of innovative flavours, and buys his ingredients as locally as possible. The egg farm is a mile away, fruit and veg travels a maximum of five miles to the pub from the farm, and this contributes to making the food fresh and keeps the standard consistently high.

Matt's sous chef Alex and part-time trainee are the only staff he has in the kitchen, cooking all the meals to order which might be over a hundred on busy summer days. "it's very important to be hands-on," says Matt, "and to understand the nature of our customers here." His passion for good food is evident in what he and Jodie chose to do with The Victory Inn, bringing a piece of Cornish history back to life for the people entwined in the story.

CORNISH MUSSELS, PRAWNS, FISH AND SQUID IN GOAN CURRY SAUCE

This dish has been on the menu at The Victory Inn since we opened in a variety of different styles. It has become a staple here; people love it and although I love to change the menu frequently, I've been told this sauce has to stay! It's very versatile, so it works with most seafood, chicken, vegetables and beans.

FOR THE CURRY PASTE

11 red chillies

5 cloves of garlic

70-100g fresh ginger, peeled

3 tbsp ground coriander

3 tbsp cumin

1 tbsp turmeric

4 whole cloves

10 dates, pitted

1 tsp salt

1 tsp sugar

8 tbsp red wine vinegar

FOR THE SEAFOOD

300g live mussels

8 tiger prawns

200g white fish

1 squid, sliced into rings

1 small onion

Dash of oil/knob of butter

1 tin of coconut milk

TO GARNISH

2 spring onions

Small bunch of fresh coriander

FOR THE CURRY PASTE

Leave one chilli aside for garnish, and put the rest into a blender or food processor along with the rest of the paste ingredients. Whizz everything together to make a smooth paste. This can be made in advance, and there will be some left over from this recipe; just pop in an airtight container and it will keep in the fridge for a couple of weeks.

FOR THE SEAFOOD

If not already cleaned, debeard the mussels and rinse them thoroughly in cold water. Chop the onion finely or in slices as preferred. Add this to the pan with a little oil or butter then add the mussels, prawns, white fish and three or four heaped tablespoons of the curry paste. Mix well to coat all the seafood and keep the contents of the pan moving, then add the tin of coconut milk. Steam over a high heat until all the mussels have opened. Any that haven't, just discard them. Finally add the squid rings and leave to cook for a further 30 seconds.

Finish by spooning the seafood and sauce into a large bowl with finely chopped spring onion, chilli and fresh coriander sprinkled over the top. Serve with fresh baguettes or focaccia for dipping.

Preparation time: 25 minutes | Cooking time: 5-10 minutes | Serves: 2-4

DIRECTORY

THESE GREAT BUSINESSES HAVE SUPPORTED THE MAKING OF THIS BOOK;
PLEASE SUPPORT AND ENJOY THEM.

CASTAWAYS

Mylor Yacht Harbour
Falmouth
Cornwall
TR11 5UF
Telephone: 01326 377710
Website: www.castawaysmylor.com

Harbourside restaurant and bar serving the very best local produce, changing with the seasons.

CHARLIE'S CAFÉ & DELI

14th Century Cottage
Fore Street
Tintagel
Cornwall
PL34 0DA
Telephone: 01840 779500
Website: www.charlies.cafe

The freshest food, the warmest welcome.

DUCHY OF CORNWALL NURSERY

Cott Road
Lostwithiel
Cornwall
PL22 0HW
Telephone: 01208 872668
Website: www.duchyofcornwallnursery.co.uk

Award-winning café full of Cornish and home-grown produce, alongside a beautifully stocked plant nursery, glasshouse and stylish shop, all with stunning views over the Fowey valley to Restormel Castle and beyond.

DUKE STREET CAFÉ

6 Duke Street
Newlyn
TR18 5JA
Telephone: 01736 368000
Website: www.dukestreetcafe.co.uk

Come visit us and enjoy a warm welcome, good coffee, breakfasts, lunches or indulge in some homemade afternoon cakes. Open Monday-Saturday 9-4pm and Sundays 10-12:30pm.

EDIE'S KITCHEN

10 Beach Road
Carlyon Bay
PL25 3PH
Telephone: 01726 813888
Website: www.edieskitchen.co.uk

Family-run cosy café serving brunch and lunch as well as an elegant bistro in the evenings.

FURNISS OF CORNWALL

Druids Road
Redruth
Cornwall
TR15 3RH
Telephone: 01209 202840
Website: www.furniss-foods.co.uk

Furniss is the oldest and most cherished Cornish biscuit brand, creating unique and exceptional biscuits since 1886.

GYLLY BEACH LTD

Cliff Road
Falmouth
Cornwall
TR11 4PA
Telephone: 01326 312884
Website: www.gyllybeach.com

Café situated right on Gyllngvase Beach popular for classic seaside lunches, contemporary evening dining and local ice cream, with a unique bakery and takeaway.

LEWINNICK LODGE

Pentire Headland
Newquay
TR7 1QH
Telephone: 01637 878117
Website: www.lewinnicklodge.co.uk

Boutique clifftop hotel, bar and restaurant, offering luxury rooms and world inspired cuisine.

PENROSE KITCHEN

Penrose Water Gardens
School Hill
Shortlanesend
Truro TR4 9ES
Telephone: 01872 225697
Website: www.penrosekitchen.co.uk

Elemental countryside dining focusing on local produce with a nod to nose-to-tail.

PHILPS BAKERY LTD

1 East Quay
Hayle
Cornwall
TR27 4BJ
Telephone: 01736 755661 (shop)
01736 753343 (office)
Website: www.philpspasties.co.uk

Family-run bakery with seven shops across Cornwall, baking fresh pasties true to tradition using top quality local ingredients.

THE PLUME OF FEATHERS

Mitchell
Newquay
Cornwall
TR8 5AX
Email: theplume@hospitalitycornwall.com
Website: www.theplumemitchell.co.uk

16th century Cornish coaching inn, offering luxury rooms and cuisine created with local and homegrown produce.

POLGOOTH INN

Rickets Lane
Polgooth
Nr St Austell
Cornwall
PL26 7DA
Telephone: 01726 74089
Website: www.polgoothinn.co.uk
Email: enquiries@polgoothinn.co.uk

A classic old Cornish village pub set in a beautiful rural valley between St Austell and Mevagissey.

THE RISING SUN

Mitchell Hill
Truro
Cornwall
TR1 1ED
Telephone: 01872 240003
Website: www.therisingsuntruro.co.uk

A true gastropub, seamlessly marrying locally sourced, sophisticated yet familiar food in a welcoming authentic pub environment.

SCOTT AND BABS WOOD FIRED FOOD LIMITED

The Barn
Retorrick Mill
Mawgan Porth
Newquay
Cornwall
TR84BH
Telephone: 01637 861746.
Website: www.scottandbabs.com

Wood fired food in a barn, on a farm!

SILCO SEAROOM

1 Wharf House
The Wharf
St Ives
Cornwall
TR26 1PG
Website: www.stivesliquor.co
Telephone: 01736 794325
Email: info@stivesliquor.co

The home of St Ives Liquor Company: a lively beachside gastrobar in the heart of St Ives. Eat, Drink, Shop.

ST IVES FARMERS' MARKET

The Guildhall
Street-an-Pol
St Ives
Cornwall
TR26 2DS
Website: www.stivesfarmersmarket.co.uk
Email: info@stivesfarmersmarket.co.uk

Open 9:30am-2pm, every Thursday throughout the year, selling local produce from fresh food to crafts produced in St Ives and the surrounding area.

TALL SHIPS CREAMERY

The New Weighbridge
Charlestown Road
Charlestown
Cornwall
PL25 3NJ
Telephone: 01726 65444
Website: www.tallshipscreamery.co.uk

Award-winning luxury handmade Cornish ice creams and sweet treats, made with love in every scoop by Victoria and her team in Charlestown.

TREWIDDEN GARDENS TEAROOM

Buryas Bridge
Cornwall
TR20 8TT
Telephone: 01736 364275
Website: www.trewiddengarden.co.uk

Proper food made with Cornish ingredients and a welcoming atmosphere in a hidden gem of a tearoom within the beautiful Trewidden Garden.

UPPERDECK BAR AND RESTAURANT

Falmouth Yacht Marina
Falmouth
TR112TD
Telephone: 01326 313481
Website: www.upperdeckfalmouth.com

Friendly and welcoming place for everyone, from families to four-legged friends: come and relax at the UpperDeck!

THE VICTORY INN

St Mawes
Cornwall
TR25DQ
Telephone: 01326 270324
Website: www.victoryinn.co.uk

Locals' pub and foodie destination, recently restored to its former place at the heart of St Mawes. Find us on all social media platforms @Victorystmawes to keep up to date.

OTHER TITLES AVAILABLE

The Little Book of Cakes & Bakes

Featuring recipes and stories from the kitchens of some of the nation's best bakers and cake-makers.
978-1-910863-48-0

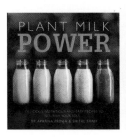

Plant Milk Power

How to create your own delicious, nutritious and nourishing moo-free milks and smoothies.
978-1-910863-41-1

Tasty & Healthy

Eating well with lactose intolerance, coeliac disease, Crohn's disease, ulcerative colitis and irritable bowel syndrome.
978-1-910863-36-7

Vegan North Cook Book

A celebration of the amazing vegan food & drink in the north of England.
978-1-910863-40-4

Sweet Chilli Friday

Simple vegetarian recipes from our kitchen to yours.
978-1-910863-38-1

RECENT TITLES FROM OUR 'GET STUCK IN' SERIES

The Edinburgh and East Coast Cook Book

features Masterchef winner Jamie Scott at The Newport, Fhior, Pickering's Gin, Pie Not, Stockbridge Market and much more.
978-1-910863-45-9

The Glasgow and West Coast Cook Book

features The Gannet, Two Fat Ladies, The Spanish Butcher, Hutchesons City Grill, Gamba and much more.
978-1-910863-43-5

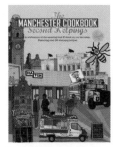

The Manchester Cook Book: Second Helpings

features Ben Mounsey of Grafene, Hatch, Refuge, Masons, Old School BBQ Bus and much more.
978-1-910863-44-2

The Derbyshire Cook Book: Second Helpings

features Chris Mapp at The Tickled Trout, Chatsworth Farm Shop, Michelin-starred Fischer's, Peacock and much more.
978-1-910863-34-3

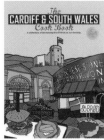

The Cardiff & South Wales Cook Book

features James Sommerin of Restaurant James Sommerin, Cocorico Patisserie, Sosban and much more.
978-1-910863-31-2

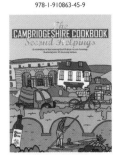

The Cambridgeshire Cook Book: Second Helpings

features Mark Abbott of Midsummer House, The Olive Grove, Elder Street Café and much more.
978-1-910863-33-6

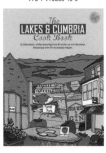

The Lakes & Cumbria Cook Book

features Simon Rogan's L'Enclume, Forest Side, Hawkshead Relish, L'al Churrasco and much more.
978-1-910863-30-5

The Nottingham Cook Book: Second Helpings

features Welbeck Estate, Memsaab, Sauce Shop, 200 Degrees Coffee, Homeboys, Rustic Crust and lots more.
978-1-910863-27-5

The South London Cook Book

features Jose Pizzaro, Adam Byatt from Trinity, Jensen's Gin, LASSCO, Salt and Pickle, Chadwicks and much more.
978-1-910863-27-5

The Essex Cook Book

features Daniel Clifford, Thomas Leatherbarrow, The Anchor Riverside, Great Garnetts, Deersbrook Farm, Mayfield Bakery and much more.
978-1-910863-25-1

All our books are available from Waterstones, Amazon and good independent bookshops.

Find out more about us at www.mezepublishing.co.uk